Performance Measurement and Control

Research and Practice

edited by

Bob Berry and David Otley

Chartered Institute of Management Accountants
63 Portland Place
London W1N 4AB

First published in 1996 by:

The Chartered Institute of Management Accountants

ISBN 1 874784 50 7

The publishers of this book consider that it is a worthwhile contribution to discussion, without necessarily sharing the views expressed, which are those of the authors.

No responsibility for loss occasioned to any person acting or refraining from action as a result of any material in this publication can be accepted by the authors or publishers.

Contents

Executive Summary

The papers in this volume are revisions of a selection of presentations made at a conference on Performance Measurement and Control organised by the Chartered Institute of Management Accountants. The aim of the conference was to encourage academics and practitioners to meet and discuss current academic research. The selection of papers for presentation at the conference and for inclusion in this volume was made by the two editors.

A large numbers of papers was submitted for possible presentation and inclusion, and we have inevitably been selective. A major aim has been to indicate the range of topics and approaches which fit within the performance measurement and control framework. The papers in this volume indicate the role which both qualitative and quantitative research approaches can play. They highlight the common measurement and control themes which appear, whether the issue is improving the performance of bank branches, setting staff remuneration packages, or improving the quality of marketing activity.

The papers have been revised in the light of comments made by the audience at the conference, so the reader has access, in part at least, to what happened on the day. Discussion was lively, and the resulting papers reflect that! To the editors a key feature of both papers and discussion was the acknowledgement that a mechanistic approach to performance measurement and control was inappropriate for systems which involve people. The following statements came through clearly:

1. Measuring an aspect of performance causes people to pay attention to it.

2. Using that measure as a control tool changes behaviour.

3. Behaviour often changes in unanticipated ways as well as in anticipated ways.

4. Therefore measurement and control systems need monitoring and revision.

While the content of many of the papers, and the link with CIMA, highlights the importance of financial control mechanisms, discussion at the conference emphasised the importance of the overall control system. There are many ways of achieving a particular result; an organisation can share the control task among different formal and informal systems in a variety of ways. Financial control systems are not the only way of achieving good financial performance.

Establishing and repairing control systems can be expensive, and complexity can add to cost. For example, it is possible to control the cost of energy use within an organisation by establishing a system of metering. Precise measures become available at regular intervals. They can be translated into financial terms and fed back to managers. But such metering systems are costly to purchase and maintain. Without further investment they tend to be fixtures whose layout does not change as factory layout changes. They continue to produce measures but not for the new activities and new areas into which the factory has expanded. An extreme alternative approach to the control of energy cost might be to buy some signs saying 'Switch off! Energy costs money', and back them up with a, frequently revamped, staff awareness campaign. This less formal system will, of course, still cost money, will still need monitoring, and will still require revision to remain effective.

One of these two energy control systems emphasises formal measurement while the other emphasises informal control. In the right circumstances each could be adequate. There is no single, best practice, performance measurement and control system, suitable for all circumstances, as the reader of this volume will find out.

Bob Berry and *David Otley*

Facing the Future: The New Internal Strategy and the New Management Accounting

Dr Rolland Munro
(Keele University)

This paper was previously presented at the CIMA conference on Performance Measurement and Control, London, 13 December 1994 and the Third Symposium on Management Control, London, July 1995. The author would like to thank participants at these meetings for a number of helpful comments and is also grateful to Simon Lilley, David Otley, Derek Purdy and Hugh Willmott.

Facing the Future: The New Internal Strategy and the New Management Accounting

Introduction

Why do managers appear, endlessly, to stress change? Improvement and change, quality and change, global competitiveness and change, empowerment and change. The implication of this emphasis on change is that extant ways of doing things have become 'out of date'. So much so, that when a new management group takes over it has become a convention for existing procedures to become rubbished as 'old'; and, hence, labelled ineffective. Existing procedures are depicted as belonging to a past management regime and, as such, should now be jettisoned. So a 'rubbishing' of present procedures *as* old, helps pave the way for an acceptance of changes to strategy, structure and systems. But more is at stake.

Attempts at 'business process reengineering', TQM, or 'corporate culture' programmes go beyond a hasty insertion of 'new' systems; or, indeed, of new managers 'making their mark'. There appears to be also a sustained attempt to dump the past and to abandon tradition. Within the factory, the hospital, the office and the university, culture has come increasingly to be seen as a 'drag' (*Strathern*, 1993). Why is this? Why has 'slagging off the past' become an integral part of managerial agendas? And, as 'change agendas', why do the target areas of quality, time management, team-building and accountability stretch pervasively across 'old' divisions: manufacturing and service, public and private, professional and unskilled?

In an earlier analysis of Worldbest, a leading UK company with world-wide sales, we tended to disregard constant references by interviewees to failings and inadequacies of the 'old' company.[1] Intent, as we were, on studying relations between the 'new' strategy and the 'new' management accounting, we were already complicit in this practice of rubbishing the past. I remember at the time being vaguely irritated at what I took to be an unnecessary harping back to, and dismissal by managers of, what was deficient before. And it seemed hardly necessary; for, at least in this particular company's case, the image of forging a 'new' company was not simply a case of the emperor's new clothes.

As we shall discuss below, some of the systems being introduced were novel, not only to this company but, at the time, to any UK company. But too hard an insistence on new systems relies overmuch on an 'instrumental' view – a detaching of the economic from the social which all too easily overlooks the *effects* of a seemingly endless import of 'new' systems. So, in this new paper, I want to suggest how a rubbishing of the past is much more than a slur on the previous regime, paving the way for systems designed to tighten control. I want, instead, to explicate the importance of viewing managerial agendas in the interpretative framework of image-making.

Images of companies do not offer themselves as mirrors of practice, as maps, so much as these images are *expressive*. The point is that, whatever their instrumental presentation, strategy, structure or systems are expressive because they both advertise managerial agendas and are advertising of these agendas. So, while images are effects, they also have effects. The 'rhetoric' surrounding concrete changes, therefore, is not detachable from any instrumental impact. As I shall illustrate, a 'new' rhetoric offers managers a new set of *moves* (*Munro*, 1993), both to make on employees and to make on each other.

In investigating a 'rubbishing' of the past in Worldbest, therefore, the paper goes on to discuss how images that are put in play act as *resources* which can be drawn upon by managers to act upon other managers. Rubbishing the past, as I shall argue, can be better understood as part of a *discourse effect*, one that is directed at managers' identity-making. Understood as discourse, these effects are not without their disciplinary consequences, especially in terms of unsettling loyalties and in accomplishing a general lowering of resistance to central direction.

The study

The study took place in a large UK manufacturing group, Worldbest, during the second year following its take-over by Goodadverts. Worldbest is regarded as the industry price-leader, with the great majority of its sales being world-wide. The focus of the paper is not, however, to enumerate all the specific effects of changes to business policy, production, personnel management and accounting, as if these are separate disciplines. Rather, the aim is to detail links between these areas.

At the beginning of the study, we were principally interested in the explicit links being made between the 'new' management accounting systems being developed and the 'intended strategy'; that is, the company strategy as understood and enunciated by top managers. In the light of our later studies in other companies and in other institutions within the public sector, this focus changed and, in this paper, we try to reassess the changes being made in Worldbest in the context of historical developments.

As we understand it now, the changes being brought into Worldbest reflect much wider agendas that we were aware of at the time. Before turning to the main analysis, however, it is perhaps helpful to set out some of the main changes under their traditional headings of structure, strategy and systems.

Organisational structure

First, we begin with organisational structure. This appeared to us to be the most important and interesting of the changes. Whereas, previously, marketing and production had been organised by product, the structure of the new groups was reorganised around a *functional* split. Essentially, production was 'decoupled' from marketing:

> *'In the brand companies there was a direct link to the market within the plant as sales and production were in the same plant. But the direct link has now been decoupled.'* *(Group purchasing manager)*

As the plant director saw it: 'Goodadverts has sliced the company from vertically integrated to horizontal'. This, as we shall see, overdramatises the matter. At the time this emphasis appeared to be a radical shift against mainstream thinking, which still espoused integrating production and marketing within product groups.

In its new structure, the group was made up of three units: manufacturing, planning and marketing. The function of planning had been added late, only two months before our arrival, and reflected difficulties in co-ordinating due to acute problems in forecasting. The last unit, marketing, somewhat confusingly, is called 'purchasing':

> *'The plan is in place for Worldbest to co-ordinate the manufacturing, planning and purchasing by dividing responsibility into Master planning, Plant manager and Quality control & purchasing.'*
> *(Group finance director)*

So a little care is necessary here. The reasons for calling marketing and sales 'purchasing' will become clearer below. For the moment, calling the marketing and sales function 'purchasing' can be understood as reflecting the type of thinking we were later to find within the reorganisation of the NHS. In the reorganisation of the NHS, pseudo-markets have been created by distinguishing between the Trusts as 'providers' and the government and their delegates as 'purchasers'.

As Trust managers have come to find out, the relations are not one of symmetry. In a phrase that has come to resonate over the years, purchasing is perceived as being 'closer to the customer'. At the time of the study, this emphasis had important consequences for Worldbest. For example, the purchasing arm of the group was given central control, reflecting their downstream position as marketing and sales:

> *'The function has centralised control and sets standard costs of glass etc. for the plants. It also does the contract negotiations with the suppliers.'* *(Group purchasing manager)*

The functional split – and therefore any idea of autonomy – has to be understood *simultaneously* as being accompanied by a return to a more centralised system. More of this in a moment.

Business strategy

The explicit business strategy of the group underlined this emphasis of the marketing unit 'purchasing' from production. Worldbest was no longer to be seen as just selling what was made. It was aiming to move production towards 'just in time', through an interim emphasis on 'producing to order'. This raises two marketing issues. The first issue involved a policy of buying up distribution channels:

> *'The strategy of buying and controlling the distribution network to capture the value they produce has been a priority. The strategy has seen the distributors grow from 25 per cent to 75 per cent controlled. This strategy is essential for control, stocking, ordering and the cash brought back into the business. It also provides the closeness to the customer necessary to the business.'* *(Group planning manager)*

Contrary to an earlier theme, therefore, business strategy sought to extend the group's vertical integration. At the sales and distribution end of the business, as the group purchasing manager explained, the 'strategy is to gain control of distribution'.

A second strategy involved a repositioning of products in the market. The production director saw strategy as 'rationalising brand positioning and concentrating resources in a smaller range'. The policy was justified analytically on the basis of 'better' market research:

> *'. . . we are now analysing consumer trends better, which have pointed towards the higher-volume markets growing slower and premium products growing.'* *(Group financial controller)*

The importance of this emphasis on analysing markets will become clear later, but it is not hard to see that better market research strengthens 'purchasing' (marketing) over 'providers' (production). Thus, we can see how the two strategies are linked. On the one hand, the outlets to the final markets are increasingly controlled by the marketing arm. And, on the other hand, the marketing arm is given an increasingly dominant position over production.

Reporting systems

Finally, in terms of reporting systems, plants were turned into cost centres, having previously been profit centres. That the plant director considered this to be one of the major changes is not surprising. In traditional textbook terms, such a shift implies a considerable loss of authority: the profit justification no longer exists locally to authorise shifts in cost spending patterns. Additionally, since the pattern of cost spending might be fixed elsewhere, plant managers also face a clear delimitation of autonomy.

As will also be discussed later, close attention in Worldbest is still given to budgets, but the principle change was seen to be the introduction of non-financial measures. In line with the then recent writings of *Kaplan* (1983, 1984), a new performance package of fourteen key ratios concentrated almost exclusively on physical measures rather than financial measures.

The justification offered for this shift towards non-financial measures came in terms of cost drivers:

> *'Businesses are too often driven by financial measures that may not reflect the reality of the overall key cost drivers, such as the identified CSFs [critical success factors].'* *(Group finance director)*

Of interest to us at the time was the introduction of different criteria, 'core values', as criteria on which shifts to cost spending patterns could be argued and justified. This emphasis on 'core values' requires some further comment.

Profit, at least short-term profit as measured by accountants, was in the process of being displaced as the sole arbiter of production decisions. Other criteria, such as 'service' and 'flexibility', were being flagged up for special attention, as if these criteria existed on a level playing field. Further, each 'core value' was being backed up by the monitoring of specific ratios intended to support these as 'critical success factors'. The point, however, is not that the concepts embraced by the four critical success factors were new; one of the new 'core values', indeed, was cost. Another was quality, about which the same point can be made:

> *'In the old system, the plants were working to quality standards without necessarily knowing it or being able to measure it. Now the concept is Total Quality. The basic question is why consumers should pay more for this type of product.'* *(Plant director)*

The key point is that where the criteria are measured, arguments over quality can compete with arguments over cost minimisation. As we shall see, however, other things are also changing here.

Rubbishing the past

The picture as set out above is more or less how we interpreted Worldbest's strategy, structure and systems seven years ago. What I wish to do now is go back to the way in which that material was presented. That is, instead of relying on an 'instrumental' view of management change, my present focus is on explicating ways in which people's commitments were mobilised. In another way of speaking, rather than dismissing the 'form' from the 'content' of change, I am trying to add it back.

The narrative which carried the instrumental changes was one of 'rubbishing' the past. More precisely, the narrative device is to conflate extant material and procedures with a notion of 'the past'. It treats any mode of ordering deployed by the previous management regime as belonging *in* the past, as history, thereby 'rubbishing' it as necessarily outdated and outmoded.

The narrative was mobilised around various themes, only some of which will be identified here. First, and in line with Hegel's dictum, the very act of looking back inflates a notion of progress. But more than this, the group can be understood as giving itself a ground from which to look back. This is the image of the group joining the 'outside world':

> *'The contrast between pre-Goodadverts strategy to post-Goodadverts strategy basically centred around positioning in the outside world.'* *(Group finance director)*

The image is one of the group being ready to meet global competition, of being world-class by being *outward*-looking in terms of strategy. By thinking of itself as 'in' markets.

In contrast, the previous company is portrayed as inward-looking; as introverted, as myopic. As one interviewee expressed it: 'The plants in the old systems jus focused on cost'. Other critical success factors are portrayed as overlooked:

> *The old system had a production committee which co-ordinated production and monitored efficiency and productivity. Service and quality were not really measured.* *(Group financial controller)*

Since at the time these were matters often taken for granted, and therefore unmeasured, the focus on cost is not surprising. However, the point goes deeper. The implication is that the previous regime saw only the financial accounts. In failing to relate these to 'markets', they failed to grasp a view of Worldbest as a *business*.[2]

> *'The old system was just badly structured. It focused on an accountant's view of the world – mainly just cost – and could be used only for transfer pricing decisions and not pricing.'* (Group finance director)

This lack of a business view was held to have its consequences. The over-focus on costs left 'brands competing among each other' and, according to the group financial controller, the company was 'late in recognising the change in consumer tastes, and the change from product orientation to market orientation was late'. The implication here is that the takeover, by making possible the new structure, saved the company; presumably, we are to believe, from an extinction that was, as yet, nowhere evident in the very healthy profit and loss account.

A second theme implies that failure was already evident. At least in the eyes of the new regime, the 'old' company, with its backward-looking ways, had already allowed chaos to enter:

> *'The discipline involved in production broke down due to the reaction-only type of ordering as a result of the idle capacity in the plants.'* (Group finance director)

In not privileging the 'market', therefore, production is seen as all but collapsed. Interestingly, in this distancing of itself from the past, those disciplines that appear to focus only on the past are condemned. Accounting as backward-looking is characterised as encouraging a 'reaction-only mentality'. The failure to be proactive means that the plants were, according to the group finance director, 'allowed the luxury of developing large stocks'. Further, in a sirenesque way, accounting encourages the wrong sort of information to be collected. Presumably, in line with the central precepts of economics, 'decisions' require information which is forward-looking, not backward-looking:

> *'The past problem is that too much information had been generated and it had not been useful to the plants to base decisions on.'* (Group finance director)

The backward-looking information systems can be viewed as having bred what the group financial controller described as 'complacency and lack of order discipline'.

A third theme around which the narrative of failure is woven is that of the vacuum. This helps to sustain the story of failure and elaborate the narrative of rapid progress. Since the very possibility of progress runs alongside a conceptualising of the past *as* past, the previous way of running the company through volume and cost becomes represented as a *lack* of direction in strategy:

> *'The previous strategy can be described as directionless, more concerned with volume than covering the full range and exploring new markets.'* (Group financial controller)

Indeed, the group finance director, sent in by Goodadverts, makes the metaphor quite explicit: 'They had been responding to a vacuum of information in the past.' The vacuum is created by not thinking about 'markets'. This is, whatever else it is, a form of incitement: avoid the past, it sucks. The injunction is not to be sucked back into the old ways. If Nature abhors a vacuum, then, as managers, so should we.

The more it changes . . .

The future, then, is the only way forward. This is not only a truism, in which case it would be trite. It is a truth regime, whose injunctions help order managers about. Without the future to aim for, we would fall back into the bad old ways of the past. This would be tantamount to failure. But that, of course, is precisely what must happen, since, on anything other than an instrumental view, we never can have left the past. Mere chronology leaves us where we are. The past has to be invented before it can be detached.

Visions of the future, then, must find some way to reinclude what has been dismissed as the past. In the 'implementation' stage, that which has been excluded, rubbished, has to be brought back in. The old bogies, the 'past' sources of failure, have to be resurrected.

Chief among these bogies for Worldbest is, of course, cost. Here is a statement of the future:

> *'Worldbest's strategy – the mission – is to be the number one spirits producer in the world and the most cost-effective.'* *(Group financial controller)*

Volume and cost! The baddies promulgated by the old regime and under which the company was unable to realise its full potential. As the group purchasing manager sees the way forward, 'the objective is to rationalise suppliers and cut costs' and 'the day-to-day job is to cut costs'.

But of course this is to be a 'new' approach to costs. There is to be a 'new' management accounting. As the group financial controller captures it, 'costs and the control of them are changing to mirror long-term strategy'. Here is the newspeak on costs:

> *'Responsibility, authority and accountability are the new keys to the plant operations – in the past the plant had no responsibility or accountability to use stock-building rationale to reduce labour to lower cost base.'* *(Group finance director)*

So it turns out that the problem before the takeover was not that there was too much focus on costs. The problem was that costs weren't really looked at properly at all! In the future, if we are to believe the new managers, costs will be controlled. In a summary of a future that has yet to take place, the group finance director is happy to assert that 'costs are driven down by yearly calibrating the *transfer price* downwards – *à la* Japanese ratchet effect' (emphasis added).

Transfer pricing? Wasn't that castigated as the *only* output of the bad old information systems? Ah, yes. But of course this transfer pricing is not to be the same. As the plant director says, 'transfer pricing is the new emphasis from the standpoint of the cost centre'. The old transfer pricing was built on the old, backward-looking accounting information systems. The new transfer pricing, on which so much depends, will be based on the new forward-looking information systems. But these are yet to be built and there are some difficulties tapping into the future:

> *'In a plant with over a thousand get-ups, each requiring different components and stocks, the building up of pack costs for each product is immense.'* *(Plant director)*

With 5,000 different variations in a leading brand and with 200 different markets, colonising the future in the name of 'markets' could prove expensive.

The problem with the future seems to arise over information requirements. These spiral in ways that are reminiscent of those 'wasteful' practices of the old cost accounting-regimes:

> *'They are in the process of building up a database with invoices encoded where the profit on every order can be calculated instantly. The marketing strategy is to increase their information technology level, with reliance on the plant to get the cost right.'* *(Group purchasing manage)*

Luckily there is a way out from the spiralling costs. It is called the past. Here is how the past is reintroduced:

> *'The budgeting method ideally begins with sales estimates, but it is a chicken-and-egg problem in that they need some idea of plant availability. In reality, the estimates are built up from past volumes with input from the sales side in terms of promotion changes, etc.'* *(Plant director)*

Then back to the future. As the production director adds 'but there is no real check on the transfer price'. The future, as marked out, continually disappoints. No wonder 'progress' is made compulsory!

Managing change

How, then, is the future to be made an obligatory passage? This is the issue to which I now turn. In the next two sections, it is mainly the changes to the 'institutional' arrangements within Worldbest that are discussed. In the penultimate section, I draw more attention to how these changes affect the 'individual' manager.

Talk of managing change appears central to attempts to colonise the future. Certainly, the production director saw his main function as being a 'manager of change', with his main responsibility being that of 'facilitating a culture change'. Nevertheless, despite the fashionable form of words, he saw this responsibility in traditional terms:

> *'The problem that makes culture establishment so important is a distrust by the labour force after the takeover.'* *(Production director)*

In particular, he suggested that contract labour was 'very suspicious'. In this respect, the production director viewed his job as that of 'lowering friction' and getting everyone 'moving towards the same goals'. Establishing the 'proper culture' to do this he expected to take 'some years'.

All this, of course, has become familiar stuff. It is a view of corporate culture that is grist to a mill that sees management obsessed with the extraction of surplus from labour. For these researchers, the notion of 'changing culture' hardly begins to get off the ground as anything other than the latest of a series of devices to increase profit. And this view is made all the more telling when the production director reveals that he wishes to 'establish a style enabling communication', seeing 'lunches with a cross-section of the labour force' as being 'critical in establishing this'. Other methods mentioned were long-service awards, single-status canteens and chiropodist visits. The more it changes, the more it remains the same. One could hardly hope to find a better example of the emperor's new clothes!

Some sense of belonging, some 'pride' in work, is clearly being identified as something to be put back in place. Back in place now that the post-takeover 'cost-cutting measures are almost exhausted'. However, it should not be thought that the production director is necessarily attempting to re-establish *traditional* loyalties within Worldbest. If so, his understanding is very different from others who are also present.

In particular, the key person imposed by Goodadverts saw things quite differently. Yes, he too saw some merit in establishing the 'cultural systems that infuse, for example, shop floor pride'. But, in stark contrast he stresses the importance of *loosening-up* traditional loyalties:

> *'. . . the old style was brand loyalty and the I-work-for-(famous name) attitude.'*
> *(Group finance director)*

Loyalty, and the pride that rests with tradition, is reduced to the status of an *attitude.* A problem. A barrier to progress. A clinging to the past. Tradition, Culture, Loyalty, these are the enemies of managerialism. As stated earlier, this same person, introduced by Goodadverts to 'put the ship on course', held the view that 'Responsibility, Authority and Accountability are the new keys to the plant operations'.

In the way that the group finance director expresses it, this might seem all old stuff. Critique, too, has a habit of rubbishing things as 'not being new'. But in the juxtaposition of placing loyalty *against* accountability, there is arguably something different from other, older patterns in discourse. Who should one account to but one's friends, one's kith and kin? How should one account but with reference to tradition and established custom? But are these matters still true?

A central effect of rubbishing the past is an implicit attack on tradition, an unsettling of loyalties. But the goal is not to rubbish these altogether. The managers of change are not to be mistaken for Utopia builders. There is no 'vision' of the future on which to build. The centre, at least in this respect, has to be understood as empty. The goal, I suggest, lies elsewhere: the attempt is to break relations between individual 'accounts', as explanations, as justifications, from 'culture', as tradition, as custom. The effect is to cut off forms of 'account-giving', the giving of reasons, explanations and justifications, from the 'resources' of tradition and custom. In rubbishing the past, the managers of change weaken the claims of tradition and custom *as* resources for account-giving. By treating 'explanations' as 'excuses', managers can prohibit each other from 'looking back'.

The change agendas of the new managerialism, the new internal strategy, are not only, as *Munro* (1994a) suggests, about a 'dissemination' of accountabilities: putting a break in the line over responsibility, so that the buck can no longer run back up the hierarchy. It is also about *colonising* accountabilities in ways that denude 'loyalties' from a giving of accounts. The new managerialism seeks a giving of accounts that excludes tradition. It is *indifferent* to the past, stories of what has happened. The new manager can 'hear what you say', but she or he cannot listen to excuses. As *Munro* (1994b) expresses the matter, only the reassurance 'it will never happen again' penetrates. And then only once . . .

Creating the internal market

In its rewriting of accountability, 'the market' is more than a model and key exemplar, it is that which is being constructed. This is particularly true of the 'internal market'. Retrospectively, the creation of internal markets is an obvious way of understanding what was going on in Worldbest. The creation of pseudo-markets, as many researchers now understand, is the key effect of erecting a functional division between purchasers and providers.

The advertising of strategy, structure and systems as 'new' were aimed precisely at putting the plants in a 'bidding system' for investment funds. As the group finance director saw it, part of the strategy is to develop a coherent 'product configuration strategy' that would 'basically involve three methods':

1. *higher investment to make moving volume between plants more flexible;*
2. *moving current volume between plants; and*
3. *taking out capacity by reducing the workforce or closing the plant down.* *(Group finance director)*

Here 'flexibility' is being described as one of Worldbest's core values. However, the 'product configuration strategy' has to be understood as being directed at creating the conditions of possibility for an internal market.

It is important to see, therefore, that, in terms of the 'new' functional structure of purchasers and providers, 'flexibility' is running all one way. It is all on the side of the purchasers, those who represent 'markets'. For production, the future is much less flexible. They have to incorporate the flexibility into themselves, so that they can jump when needed. Whereas before they could refuse orders, or delay meeting them, now plant managers are more closely boxed into meeting the order.

If they are given the order at all! For the core value of flexibility also has the effect of heightening uncertainties over when purchases will be asked for; or on what conditions they will be granted. Fail to respond quickly enough to 'purchasing' – which is not yet instantly, for 'lead time agreements is a new concept' – and purchasing will go elsewhere. If a plant lacks the 'movable volume' to cater to changes in demand, then purchasing will go elsewhere. This, as will be discussed shortly, has serious consequences, since production's ability to meet the budget is almost entirely dependent upon purchasing's estimates of orders materialising. Nor can a plant manager, as in the 'old' system, rely on having spare capacity to meet orders. The instructions are clear: fail to get costs down, by, say, taking out capacity, and we close you down.

The same picture of an asymmetry in relations between the purchaser and the provider becomes clear when quality is re-examined. In this respect it is of some interest to return to an earlier quote:

'In the old system, the plants were working to quality standards without necessarily knowing it or being able to measure it. Now the concept is Total Quality. The basic question is why consumers should pay more for this type of product.' *(Plant director)*

On further analysis, the apparent *non sequitur* between the last two sentences turns out to be just the good business sense of the new regime. The commitment to quality within production and the commitment to give value added to the customer are intimately connected. Total quality is a philosophy of 'cost down' – the message is to get costs down without affecting quality.

Here is where the asymmetry comes into play. Only one side gets to argue *for* quality – the 'purchaser'.[3] For the other side, the provider, quality is a matter of bringing in 'best practice', where best practice is always going to have to be the cheapest way of delivering to product specification:

'One of the key philosophies in driving down the costs involved is examining the "best demonstrated practices" within their plants and outside.' *(Group finance director)*

By forcing the supplier to 'self-certify', the burden of accountability is turned inwards and any tendency to 'try it on' is held in check by expectations that are always returning to 'zero'.

Facing the future

Notions of the market are being turned against the traditional institutions, the hospital, the local council, the academy. But this is not, as some may fear, in order to obliterate them. Why lose existing forms of control? Once each is in the form of a 'new' province of quality' (*Munro*, 1994a), these institutions can be expected to have their place. Once freed from the tyranny of the past, of a solidarity that respects only habit, tradition and custom, these too are ready to be part of the future.

The surprise is rather to find such similar notions of the market being turned against institutions in the private sector. But as it turns out, many of the problems, such as those of estimating costs, are the same. The difficulty is that companies like Worldbest so straddle the world that, through horizontal and vertical integration, markets have disappeared 'inside'. As we have seen with Worldbest, their claim to serve 'markets' has to be constructed through specific devices, such as that of creating a 'functional' split within the empire.

Notions of the market, *as* the 'outside world', *as* 'business', *as* 'reality', are being directed at institutions. All institutions. But to stop here is to miss the point. I am arguing that the importance of these notions arises as a consequence of their being turned on persons. Destroy the different images of the institution in ways that ensure that no-one wants to belong to *that.*

Persons, note, not 'individuals'. The concept of the 'individual', which is at the heart of the thinking of the New Right, is still in its making. What, crucially, is at stake in extending the rhetoric over 'autonomy' and 'choice' into the workplace is a *making-up of identity*. Loyalty, tradition and custom are being rubbished as backward-looking, as 'the past'. If I am right, then it follows that the target of change agendas must be the 'carrier' of these viruses, the person as someone prone to 'belonging', the person as a *set of traditional affiliations*.

Like everything else that is branded as being in the past, however, identity-*making* cannot simply be left behind. As if it really were in the past! If it is their disposition, people will continue trying to belong. Only previous *identities* can be broken. This, I propose, is the implication behind the rhetoric of 'managing change'. Never to let identities become settled. *To keep belonging on the move*.

The truth of this proposal cannot be evidenced here. Of course, there is considerable material I could draw on to show how the introduction of 'flexibility' into the labour force, and also to middle managers, helps split their loyalties. But the questions I am raising are not strictly matters of truth, at least in the sense of empirical tests. In understanding 'change' it matters little whether there is one example or a thousand.

Nor, it should be emphasised, are the relevant empirical examples necessarily in the form of *either* an institution *or* an individual. Rather, I am surmising that we may have been misunderstanding the very 'entities' that are undergoing change. As researchers of 'organisations' we have a tendency to look at changes 'within' the organisation, or 'to' the institutional fabric; and only then think about the 'behavioural' effects on people. But this is to already atomise persons as *individuals*.

In contrast to the sociological fuss made about change at an institutional or an organisational level, I am suggesting that the current emphasis on change is a nexus between persons and their affiliates: how 'we' network in order to make ourselves up as 'we'. So, in the terms adopted by *Latour* (1987), the theoretical device of 'blackboxing' persons as 'individuals' appears to be inappropriate for understanding institutional change, and in the final section of this paper I want to bring these different perspectives together.

The future as obligatory passage

In order to illustrate how accountability is being realigned within Worldbest, it is helpful to fill in some details of three 'control technologies', the importance of which we overlooked in our first analysis. The first technique, 'cascade', is treated in the managerialist literature as if it were 'new'. However, it is, in some crucial respects, a version of the very 'old' techniques of 'top-down' management (see also *Knights and Willmott*, 1987; *Roberts*, 1980). The second technique is that of using performance management systems for management selection. Like the third technique I examine, extending employment practices, this is so 'old' that we simply took its importance for granted. Each of these three techniques is interlocking and will be discussed in turn.

Cascade

Techniques of cascade are usually linked to the idea of top managers 'communicating' strategy and, in this respect, are usually sold on the idea of the efficiency of their transmission. This is patently false. Since they are built around the device of hierarchy, the cascade, there is no reason to think that they could be any more effective than 'traditional' communication channels.

As it turns out, strategy was not 'communicated' but, as in the espionage field, was given out as if on a 'need-to-know' basis:

> *'The link with Goodadverts' strategy is unknown, except that Goodadverts is always driving for efficiency to drive cost down.'* *(Group financial controller)*

This appears as a pattern of deletion: some knowledge is given, but always on the basis that there is 'more' strategy not passed on. Here the cascade is essential to preserving this possibility:

> *'Specifically, a presentation was made by Harry Cohen [managing director] at Poshhotel. Meetings with Gerrie Most [boss] in the future will ensure that the strategy as dictated from the top achieves the* filtration *process.'* *(Group financial controller, emphasis added)*

The production director also said he was relatively unaware of the strategy of Goodadverts, the new owners:

> *'The strategy is implicitly discussed. The way it is communicated is by briefings from Harry Cohen [managing director] three to four times a year. The briefings are disseminated by breaking down into work groups, to the front-line manager, then to the shop floor, to the men on how they are doing.'* *(Plant director)*

And again, on to plant level the result of the cascade is the same:

'The strategy does not get to the plants directly. A limited amount of strategy is communicated to the plant in briefings.' (Production director)

The 'cascade' allows for a process of *deletion* that, at each level, preserves an ambiguity in respect of overall strategy.

The importance of conserving this ambiguity is hard to overestimate. Before continuing, let us remember how far the manager has come. With the past rubbished, his or her knowledge base is cut off. When it comes to giving accounts, such as giving reasons for budget variances, these must be future-oriented. But virtually the *only* resource for this is a knowledge of strategy.

So this is where asymmetrical relations arise. Through a cascade of strategy, the less senior manager at each level is positioned *as if* they know less than the superior manager. This may or may not be true. Nevertheless, as long as each manager believes it to be true, the power effect of bolstering hierarchy will be the same. In respect of strategy, therefore, it hardly matters whether senior managers actually knew more than they said. Rather, the imputations by their subordinates that they always *do* know more provide a firm basis on which the senior manager can, retrospectively, interpret results. This is the crucial tie to performance management systems.

Performance management systems

The detail surrounding performance management systems was presented blandly enough. The performance management system:

'. . . is still in the development stage and is essentially an MBO approach for identifying key management succession people, movement, activities etc.' (Group finance director)

Perhaps the only significant part of this statement is the stress on the relations between performance management systems and matters such as that of succession. The difference from what went before is vital. No longer are financial rewards, such as bonus, tied explicitly and perhaps only to financial performance. It is important to see that both sides of the equation are now extended: on the one side, the whole gamut of rewards is apparently 'up for grabs'; and, on the other side, a whole range of 'new' factors is being opened up by the co-existence of four critical success factors. If management by objectives was once sold on the basis that it reduced ambiguity, this variation is a leap in the opposite direction. Quantity or quality? Cost or flexibility? Ambiguity looks to have been made rampant.

Well, not quite. Only for some. Within Worldbest, as we have seen, interpretability will be all on the one side: the side of the 'purchaser'. So in thinking of relations between managers in the line, something else is changing. An 'internal market' is appearing here at each stage in the line. On the one side the budget holder as 'purchaser'; on the other side the budgetee as 'provider'. The complexities here will take a moment to explicate.

One interpretation of an extended range of performance measures is that one variable 'counts' more than any of the others. And this was one view:

'Certainly the budget is the heaviest weighting in performance evaluation. It focuses on cost, yes, but everything else impacts on the budgeted costs.' (Plant director)

Repeating that the budget 'provides a key measure of success', the plant director added that 'better information can be obtained'. But this 'better information' is, as we have seen, awaiting the information systems of the future. Thus, failing these, other modes of interpretation can be called upon:

'. . . at the moment gut feel still plays a large part in deciding what is successful.' (Production director)

So here again the superior gets to decide how to read results. And this is a system which is sufficiently justifiable to offer a deferral of the future:

> *'I'm sceptical about having narrowly defined the objectives, as it can lead to just focusing on those being measured precisely instead of tackling the real problems.'* *(Plant director)*

Perhaps all this reads like a return to the systems of the past? But it isn't. Again, the ambiguity of interpretation is all one way. Interpretability is to be all on the side of the purchaser. Purchasers become enacted as one's superior, rather than simply holding a more senior appointment in the hierarchy.

That this already seems to be the case in most companies brings us, somewhat hastily, back to 'accounts' – the giving of reasons and explanations – to see the difference that is being produced. In one company, I might merely have to offer an explanation for, say, not meeting the budget. Take it or leave it. But, within Worldbest, I don't just offer explanations, I have to sell them. And in a particular way. Up against a manager, the purchaser, with imputations of his or her superior knowledge of strategy, and with a rubbishing of the past cutting me off from a traditional reservoir of explanations as 'excuses', this is a performance management system to make my forelock curl.

Employment practices

At work in conjunction with these controls is an equally 'old' control technology. Inclusion and exclusion. Of people. But again there is a difference. The boundaries between the inside and the outside of the organisation become more complex when some of the labour is made 'core' and some of it is 'hourly'. So flexibility, as a critical success factor, is at work here too, accomplishing divides that split loyalties. For example:

> *'. . . the idea is to gear labour to the trough and hire temps to the peaks.'* *(Group financial controller)*

However, this concept did not only apply to factory floor workers, it applied to managers and specialist staff:

> *'The philosophy also exists that special projects are better served by experts than a standing labour force.'* *(Group financial controller)*

Since the market now is as inside as it is outside, *anyone* is replaceable. It is not only employees on the shop floor, but also middle managers who are being made dispensable.

In summary, these are the three controls we overlooked in our first analysis: an imputation of superiors knowing more strategy by being further up the cascade; results that have to be read by one's boss before they are deemed to be either a success or a failure; and the flexibility for the purchaser to eliminate one's job through 'outsourcing'. Together, these are the conditions under which the future has become an obligatory passage. The provider not only begins to recognise that the only type of knowledge that counts is knowledge of what it is that the 'purchaser' wants. The provider is also entrapped into helping accomplish such arrangements.

Conclusion

Much of the drama that we overlooked in Worldbest is now being played out more noisily in the public arena. Understanding why change agendas have begun to appear so pervasively throughout society calls for research on organisations to go beyond narrow disciplinary boundaries. Certainly, it makes no sense to study something like performance management systems under a 'partition' solution which keeps management accounting, or human resource management, separate. But, similarly, studying marketing or strategy as if it was disjunct from a deployment of budgets looks equally fruitless. None of this is to say that these distinctions don't matter. Clearly they do. But explanation has to work harder when debates, previously confined to the 'private' sector, have more recently spread so far across the public sector; and when the effects which are generated can no longer be tidied into the little boxes of academic disciplines.

Overlooking the importance of a rubbishing of the past was, on reflection, perhaps no accident. Caught up in a debate over the emperor's new clothes, our sensitivities were dulled to asking what might be critical in this 'manufacturing' of a future and 'rubbishing' of the past. It has become a convention of critique, particularly in debates centred around labour process theory, to rubbish corporate changes as a re-packaging of the old product, as little more than a legitimating of the new regime. The more it changes, the more it remains the same. The new 'slim' image of organisations as 'empowering' and 'team-building' tends to be read as a mere mask on the old 'fat' image of organisations as accounting-buttressed hierarchies, passing credit upwards and blame downwards.

Changes to reporting systems are important, however, if not always in ways that we anticipate. If, in our first analysis, we misunderstood the nature of changes within Worldbest, at least we did not simply dismiss the changes being made to reporting systems as nothing new. As researchers interested in the question 'Who benefits?', our duty is to *detail* the effects of changes in reporting systems and, too often, we muff it. Here is a first ground on which much current critique of managerialism fails. Always reducing the new to old washes out differences among managerial devices to a bottom-line thinking. It is a formula that flattens all the effects of technique as being just more of the same: the extraction of 'surplus' from labour.

The importance of the systems introduced to Worldbest (and, it seems, to many organisations since) is that they are 'instrumental' in bringing in a framework of 'provider' and 'purchaser'. The introduction of this 'market' framework has become most explicit as part of the 'new' organisation of the health service. What I have tried to show in this paper is how the design of the 'new' systems, with their stress on quality and flexibility, introduces an asymmetry into these relations that is entirely necessary – if it is intended that *only* the 'purchaser' can draw on these arguments. This is not to say that these arguments, being *for* quality, or being *for* flexibility, have no resonance 'within' production. This is not something that we examined extensively in this particular study, but clearly they do. And especially so if the same relations of purchaser and provider are introduced into the factory as 'cell manufacturing', or into the hospital as 'primary nursing'.

Are being 'for' change, or being 'against' change, sufficient criteria, then, by which to justify promotion? Are they sufficient criteria by which to switch employees between the 'core' and the 'hourly'? Or even between employment and the dole? Surely not, and in the present analysis I have stressed how none of these instruments work alone. So we must be careful not to be reiterating a facile view of power as sanctions. The intricacies of the new managerialism go beyond a view that people are 'needed' to read instruments like accounting numbers. Or even that people are somehow 'needed' to speak on their behalf. What I am attempting to stress, instead, is how *prefigured* is any space that entitles persons to speak on behalf of instruments. Before they can apply sanctions, persons have to be sanctioned first *as* spokespersons.

Regrettably, we still know too little about these particular processes of affiliation and exclusion. In studying *how* change is packaged, I have attempted to dislodge the instrumental view of management and illustrate, instead, how these matters of affiliation and belonging are always at work. In particular, I hope to have shown how a stress on 'internal advertising' can make the study of systems, structure or strategy acutely interesting. Changes in internal advertising do more than suggest shifts in internal strategy. With careful analysis, they may indicate that different forms of control are in play and, with this, clarify the potential for forms of resistance. For example, managers at Worldbest were being incited to belong to the 'outside' world – a world of markets – at the very moment that markets were being created 'inside' the company through the adoption of a functional structure between 'purchasers' and 'providers'.

This, then, seems to me a second ground in which the extant critique of managerialism can be found wanting. Researchers have been too ready, on both sides, to presume that managerialism conforms to an instrumental view. But we cannot have it both ways. Either we believe in artefacts being expressive, or we don't. If we do, then we must reformulate the terms under which we understand managerialism to be working. The point is that, whatever their instrumental presentation, strategy, structure or systems are expressive because they are advertised *and* advertising. The 'rhetoric' surrounding strategy, structure or systems is not detachable from their content.

Rubbishing the past, an effect which appears to be only possible within an instrumental framework, turns out, in a different line of thinking, to be about shifting affiliations. Perceived as discourse, images set up 'permissions' (*Munro*, 1992) for employees to draw on one form of words instead of another. The discourse effect is that one form of words registers as an 'argument' and, perhaps, even 'the way forward'; while another form of words is heard as the speaker being 'resistant' to change, or as an 'excuse'. And, as one form of words takes on resonance through iteration, so another form of words can be marginalised as 'off the agenda', or silenced as 'old hat'.

In this way, a making up of 'individuals' in the organisation becomes restructured through changes in discourse. Drawing on the material from Worldbest, I have tried to explicate how this may happen. The configuration, first, of an ambiguity over strategy, where the superior appears to know 'more', and, second, an ambiguity over what counts as results in the performance management systems, where the superior has to name a failure before it is a failure, together sets up an enclosure in which cultural performance by managers will change. To 'do manager' in Worldbest, to be seen to 'deliver' in Worldbest, entails more than getting the numbers right: the right forms of words also have to be found. Whereas before, managers could talk out budget variances into 'the past', as the vicissitudes of history, now the numbers being tracked across the performance management systems have to be talked *up*, through strategy, *as* 'the future'.[4]

In this paper I have suggested how a debate between the 'past' and the 'future' not only colonises debates between quantity against quality, profit or pleasure, procedures versus flexibility, but is one that rides on their backs. On my analysis, rubbishing the past is aimed, in part, at leaving employees and managers no other ground than 'the future' on which to stand. With some hindsight from later studies, I feel we can begin to understand why change agendas configure around 'total quality', 'time management', 'team building' and 'accountability'. Unlikely as they sound, this is the very stuff of identity from which no one can stand aside. All of them institute specific *permissions* 'empowering' an individual: her right to produce quality, her right to manage her time, her right to belong to a team, her right to account. All are matters that appear to respect the individual as having 'autonomy', as a free entity with the right to choose.

Debate, then, takes place 'within' an institution. And, importantly, among 'individuals'. But discourse is no respecter of the boundaries of either institutions or individuals. Indeed, debate also takes place ostensibly *within* the 'disciplined' subject (*Roberts*, 1991). Change agendas are not aimed at altering the behaviour of 'individuals' directly. They are aimed, albeit indirectly, at the processes 'making up' identity. This, then, is another reason for taking care over questions of belonging and affiliation. Her will to autonomy, to freedom from 'action in a block', can become no more than moments of a changing performance that entraps her 'keeping up' of loyalties within an endless quest for improvement. In creating a seesaw of moral discourse, change agendas constitute resources from which a person can construct her personality as *for* quality, or *for* flexibility. *As* 'knowing her job'; or *as* 'living in the past'. And so on. The endless choices being manufactured for the self also divide and rule.

Notes

1. The research for this study was initially conducted with Perry Cooper and draws on material used in our paper, 'The Impact of Changes in Strategic Thinking on Management Control Systems: the Selection of Non-financial Measures in a Functional Structure', given at the British Accounting Association Annual Conference, Bath, March 1989. The paper was not published for reasons of confidentiality.

2. In case the matter is not obvious, it should be pointed out that a close analysis of the transcribed accounts of managers suggests a different view. Worldbest was not only run as a business. It was run as a business in the very terms that are being denied here. For example, in mentioning that plants 'had their own control meetings in the past', one interviewee remarked that: 'measures

were mainly physical rather than financial'. As has been mentioned above, the use of physical measures instead of financial was a centrepiece of the 'new' regime.

3. Product specification was seen as the main brake on plant managers using 'cost down' in order to revert to the cheapest and nastiest means of production. Specifications had to be met in a regime that had become more rigid than ever before:

   'The temptation to lower quality is counterbalanced by the quality teams, including engineers, which will take a concept developed by marketing and attempt to set specifications from the concept to implementation of ordering stage.' *(Group purchasing manager)*

   This reliance on specification could increase the burden on the 'purchaser'. It is important therefore to appreciate that this route had been cut off by transferring responsibility for all checking to the supplier:

   'The quality assurance programme is designed to make an early shift to suppliers for the onus of quality. The monitoring takes place in the form of grading suppliers in terms of scores for quality, delivery and quantity accuracy. Such monitoring drives suppliers to efficiency and Worldbest towards better scheduling. The ultimate aim is to get suppliers to self-certify.' *(Group purchasing manager)*

   In this way, the potential for erosion of accountability is held in check. Left to check for themselves, the purchaser might not always pick up 'poor quality'; or, in receiving too many defective products, they might discover the process of sorting and returning these to be too complex.

4. In that not everyone would survive happily there, it is likely that Worldbest is extreme rather than typical. In other institutions, the hospital, the council, the university, I suspect 'new' and 'old' images of organisation do not simply replace each other. The images, more likely, create an *intertextuality* for the subject between the future and the past. Different forms of accountability that provide different dangers and whose co-presence may incite a 'close reading' by members of situations that sometimes makes someone look back to 'custom' and 'precedent', and sometimes makes that same person look forward to 'strategy' and the 'way ahead'.

References

Kaplan, R. (1983), 'Measuring manufacturing performance: a new challenge for management accounting research', *The Accounting Review*, Vol. LVIII, No. 4, pp. 686–705.

Kaplan, R. (1984), 'The evolution of management accounting', *The Accounting Review*, Vol. LIX, No. 4, pp. 390–418.

Knights, D. and Willmott, H.C. (1987), 'Organizational culture as management strategy: a critique and illustration from the financial services industry', *International Studies in Management and Organisation*, XVII (3), pp. 40–63.

Latour, B. (1987), *Science in Action: How to Follow Scientists and Engineers Through Society*, Milton Keynes: Open University Press.

Munro, R. (1992), 'Enabling participative change: the impact of a strategic value', *International Studies in Management and Organization*, Vol. 21, No. 4, pp. 52–65.

Munro, R. (1993), 'Just when you thought it safe to enter the water: accountability, language games and multiple control technologies', *Accounting, Management and Information Technologies*, Vol. 3, No. 4, pp. 249–271.

Munro, R. (1994a), 'Governing the new province of quality: autonomy, accounting and the dissemination of accountability', in H. Willmott and A. Wilkinson (eds), *Making Quality Critical*, London: Routledge, 1994.

Munro, R. (1994b), 'Calling for accounts, monsters, membership work and management accounting', *Proceedings of the Fourth Interdisciplinary Perspectives on Accounting Conference*, (University of Manchester, 11–13 July 1994).

Roberts, J. (1990), 'Strategy and accounting in a UK conglomerate', *Accounting, Organizations and Society*, 15, pp. 107–126.

Roberts, J. (1991), 'The possibilities of accountability', *Accounting, Organizations and Society*, 16, pp. 355–368.

Strathern, M. (1993), 'Society in drag', *Times Higher Educational Supplement*, 2 April.

The Effect of Performance Benchmarking upon Investment Manager Attitudes to Risk

Mavis Crossland
(University of Leeds)

The author is grateful to the ESRC for financial support. The paper is part of the project, 'How the market evaluates performance and channels funds', which is itself part of the the Functioning of Markets initiative of the ESRC.

The Effect of Performance Benchmarking upon Investment Manager Attitudes to Risk

1 *Introduction*

The results presented in this study form part of a larger survey of the interface between the 'City' and the corporate sector, in which the attitudes and views of the three participant groups (fund managers, investment analysts and corporate directors) were explored. The objectives of the survey were primarily to ascertain those factors of importance in the investment decision-making of investment managers.

One central theme of the project is whether the pressures on institutional fund managers to perform satisfactorily against short-term benchmarks results in these managers adopting a correspondingly short-term approach to their investment strategies, and whether such short-term strategies influence the behaviour of corporate management. The absence of performance monitoring, with its attendant pressures, from the picture presented in mainstream finance theory, of the behaviour of 'the investor', and its very real presence in the environment in which fund managers operate, may be expected to have an effect upon the decision heuristics of the fund manager. The survey results presented here focus upon the effects of performance benchmarking upon fund manager attitudes to investment decisions.

Section 2 presents the theoretical background to the study before moving on in section 3 to consider the potential influence of the investment environment within which fund managers operate. Section 4 introduces elements drawn from the behavioural sciences in order to reach expectations of investment manager behaviour. The hypotheses to be tested and the research method employed are outlined in section 5. Finally, section 6 presents the findings of the study.

2 *Investor behaviour: the theoretical background*

The portrait of 'the investor' as presented in modern portfolio theories is that of the rational economic agent: the maximising, risk-averse,[1] lone individual, acting on his own behalf and receiving returns from his investments. Risk is considered to be the variance (or standard deviation) of return under portfolio theory or the sensitivity to market movements (the beta coefficient) under the capital asset pricing model. As risk can be decomposed into market risk and firm specific risk, and the latter can be diversified away, the only risk element of consequence to the investor, and for which a return should be expected, is (according to CAPM) market risk as denoted by the beta coefficient. Hence, under CAPM the expected return is composed of a risk-free element for time, plus a risk premium for bearing market risk, and is a linear function of the market risk (the beta coefficient) of the security or portfolio (Figure 1).

The risk-free rate (R_f) has a beta of 0 and a risk premium of 0; the market portfolio (M) has a beta of 1 and an expected risk premium of ($R_m - R_f$). Expected return is a linear function of the beta coefficient:

$$E(R_s) = R_f + [E(R_m) - R_f]\,\beta_s$$

Figure 1: The security market line

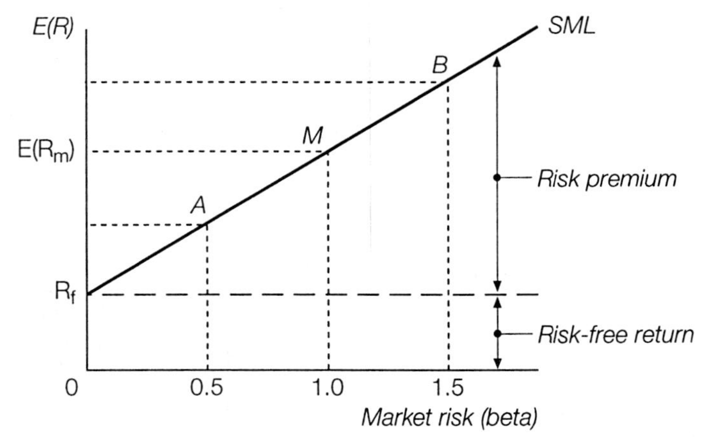

Given the assumptions relating to the nature of 'the investor' and the prescriptions of modern portfolio theories, as outlined above, two questions arise. Firstly, does the investor of theory reflect the investor of practice? Secondly, if he does not, will the divergence affect expected behaviour? In order to consider these questions, the actual investment operating environment will be surveyed, followed by a consideration of the relevant contributions from the behavioural sciences.

3 *The investment environment*

In the years from the Diamond Report of 1963 to the Philips and Drew survey of 1988, there was a marked rise in the proportion of UK equity being managed by financial institutions.[2] This share rose from 27.8 per cent of total equity holdings in 1963 to 67 per cent by 1988; that of pension funds alone rose from 7 per cent in 1963 to 32 per cent by 1988. Alongside the rise in importance of institutional holdings must be placed the corresponding decline in private investor holdings. These have fallen from a 58.7 per cent share of total equity holdings in 1963 to 18 per cent by 1988. Nor is there any reason to suspect that the trend has not continued.

The significance of this shift in holdings is that 'the investor' can no longer be characterised as the lone individual acting on his own behalf. The typical investor is now a salaried employee, working within an organisational context, and acting on behalf of others. Furthermore, the growth in recent years of the performance monitoring culture and the performance monitoring agencies has contributed to an investment industry in which performance monitoring is the norm. For example, the two performance monitoring agencies for pension fund portfolios, World Markets and Combined Actuarial Performance Services, between them probably cover almost the entire pension fund industry.[3]

The performance monitoring agency is appointed by the trustees of a pension fund in order to report on the performance of the fund in terms of both absolute return and relative performance; relative, that is, to other funds' performances. In terms of relative performance, the benchmark against which funds are measured is that of the median fund performance. Such reporting typically occurs on a quarterly basis, with individual fund managers similarly required to explain, in person, the performance of the funds under their management to trustee meetings each quarter. (The relationships of the contracting parties are set out in Figure 2.)

Given the widespread use of performance monitoring, it is hypothesised that this may affect investment behaviour. Consequently, the following section considers the contribution of certain areas drawn from the behavioural sciences in order to form expectations of investment manager behaviour.

Figure 2: The interested parties to a pension fund management contract

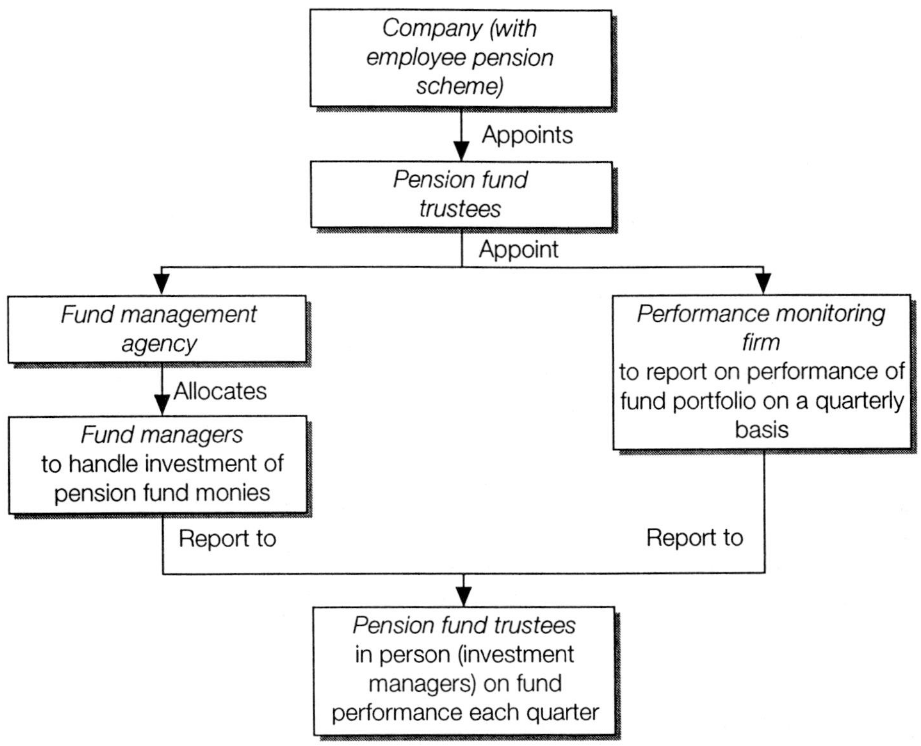

4 The contribution of behavioural science

The 'investor' of finance theories is assumed to be rational, utility maximising and risk averse: a rational economic agent. Theories of rational choice assume future preferences which are exogenous, stable and known. They therefore founder in situations of collective decision-making where there exist conflicting objectives within the group, where individual preferences are not clear and consistent, and where they change over time. Such prescriptive decision-making processes as are entailed in subjective expected utility theory (the foundation of modern portfolio theories) do not correspond to the bounded nature of real-world decision-making as, for example, *Mintzberg*'s study (1975) of managerial behaviour showed. Mintzberg concluded that the most significant decisions were made by intuitive judgement rather than by hard data analysis.

Furthermore, over recent years expected utility theory has been subjected to a barrage of empirical tests challenging the validity of the assumptions upon which it rests. The assumption that for any choice people have a definite preference (including indifference) was found to be violated in tests conducted by *Mosteller and Nogee* (1951) who found that subjects, on repeated measures of preference, would not always give the same answers. The assumption of transitivity (that is if A is preferred to B and B is preferred to C then A should be preferred to C) was found wanting by *Coombs* (1975), and by *Tversky* (1969) who found systematic and predictable violations.

The assumption of invariance of preference between certainty and risk was examined by *Kahneman and Tversky* (1979), who found that outcomes which obtained with certainty were given disproportionate weighting compared with uncertain outcomes (the certainty effect). Distortions in assessing probabilities were demonstrated by *Ellsberg* (1961) and *Maya Bar-Hillel* (1973), who found that people tend to overestimate the probability of conjunctive events and underestimate that of disjunctive events. For example, assessing the probability of dying in an aircraft crash as being higher than the combined probabilities of the crash or, given the crash, of dying.

A further area of concern is the assumption of risk aversion. *Kunreuther and Slovic* (1978), *Hershey and Schoemaker* (1980) and *Slovic et al.* (1979) found that risk dispositions exhibited (in laboratory tests) were counter to the assumed risk aversion of economic theory. Further discrepancies from the risk-aversion assumption were detected by *Kahneman and Tversky* (1979), *Schoemaker and Kunreuther* (1979), and *Fishburn and Kochenberger* (1979). They found that risk attitudes varied according to the situation presented, namely that business executives were often risk averse in gambles which could result in ruinous losses, but were risk seeking in gambles where outcomes were below target levels.

The conclusions of empirical research would indicate that, contrary to the theoretical underpinnings of modern portfolio theory, the human decision-making process is a relatively simple one based upon simple heuristics, or rules of thumb, rather than upon rigorous, systematic thinking and complex probabilistic calculations.

Of particular relevance to this study are the propositions of *Kahneman and Tversky* (1979), according to which, outcomes are perceived not in absolute terms but in relative terms; relative, that is, to a reference point. The reference point is usually formulated in terms of the *status quo*, but may be altered by the way in which the options are framed.

Furthermore, perceived gains are regarded differently from perceived losses. Where the potential outcome is perceived to be above the reference point (a potential gain) there is a disinclination to gamble away an attractive outcome (see Figure 1), that is, behaviour is risk averse. Where the potential outcome is perceived to be below the reference point (a perceived loss) behaviour becomes risk seeking. Moreover, the response to a loss is more extreme than the response to a gain of the same magnitude, as there is a greater disutility from a loss than there is from a gain of the same magnitude.

Figure 3: Kahneman and Tversky's value function

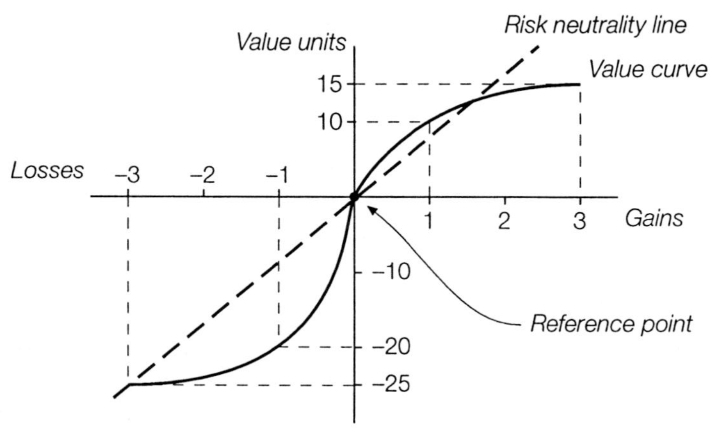

The conclusions of *Kahneman and Tversky* are well supported by empirical research carried out over the years since 1979 (see *Budescu and Weissfound*, 1987; *Fiegenbaum and Thomas*, 1988; *Kameda and Davis*, 1990).

In the context of investment decision-making by fund managers, the propositions put forward by Kahneman and Tversky would imply that potential portfolio performance outcomes will be evaluated relative to the 'reference point', that is, the benchmark portfolio return, rather than in absolute terms. A further implication is that an investment manager will attach greater importance to avoidance of a 'loss' than to achievement of a 'gain' of the same amount, and that a fund manager's attitude to risk will vary depending upon his performance relative to the benchmark. However, this presupposes that the investment manager is motivated to seek to achieve a 'good' outcome. According to *Lawler*'s (1969) Expectancy Theory, motivation to achieve a particular outcome is a function of expectation of outcome, expectation of reward and the value placed upon the reward. That is, what is the probability that the desired outcome can be achieved; what is the probability that the appropriate reward will follow the achievement of the desired outcome; and finally, what value does the individual concerned place upon the reward?

Within the context of an investment manager subject to performance monitoring, it might be expected that where performance is above the median, the expected outcome would be to keep the fund management contract, attracting a positive reward (salary, promotion, approbation, keeping job), the rewards being those which one might reasonably assume are desired (Figure 4).

Figure 4: Outcome-reward matrix

Performance	*Outcome*	*Reward*	*Valence*
Above median	Keep contract	Positive	Desired
Below median	Lose contract	Negative	Not desired

However, where performance is below median, the fund manager might expect to lose the fund contract, carrying negative consequences for himself (loss of pay, and promotion, disapprobation, loss of job), the rewards being those which might reasonably be assumed are undesirable. This raises the question with which this study is concerned: does performance benchmarking affect investment manager attitudes?

5 *Hypotheses and interview procedure*

Two null hypotheses arising from the foregoing finance theory (as presented in section 2) are:

Hypothesis 1 The investor will seek to maximise expected return for a given level of risk. He will therefore be concerned with absolute rather than relative levels of performance.

Hypothesis 2 The investor will regard the sole relevant measure of equity risk to be the sensitivity of the share or portfolio to market movements, as measured by the beta coefficient.

In order to test the null hypotheses, requests for an interview were sent to every UK mainland insurance company and investment management firm (comprising merchant banks, stock brokers and specialist investment managers). Of 121 delivered requests, positive responses were obtained from 64 institutions (a response rate of 53 per cent), and interviews were subsequently conducted with each respondent.

Before starting the interview process proper, initial interviews were held with five individuals involved in the process of appraising fund manager performance generally. These interviews were conducted on an unstructured basis and allowed the interviewees to explain how they saw the performance evaluation system currently being used in the UK. Pilot interviews were then held with four individuals involved with pension fund management or insurance company fund management. These interviews were also unstructured, and the aim was to allow the interviewees to talk about the nature of their work and the type of evaluation system under which they operated. From these initial interviews, it was possible to form a general impression of the work of fund managers and the way in which their performance was appraised and rewarded. On the basis of the interviews an interview questionnaire was drawn up, and this formed the basis of the further series of 64 structured interviews. All the interviews were taped and their contents transcribed. Responses were analysed using SPSS-PC. Frequency distributions were obtained and, where appropriate, the data was partitioned into response groups, either by type of fund managed or by type of benchmark employed. The statistical significance of the differences between response groups was tested using the Kruskal Wallis one-way analysis of variance. This tests the null hypothesis that the samples come from identical populations with respect to averages. The chi-square (χ^2) statistic is reported, as this gives a measure of the difference in answers, and the significance level.

6 *Survey findings*

Background of the sample

Table 1 provides some background details of the fund managers interviewed. The majority of the funds managed related to pension schemes: of the 64 investment managers interviewed, 41 (64.1 per cent) had a pension fund as the principal type of fund managed; the next most important group were private clients (13) followed by life assurance (7) and unit or investment trusts (3). The most frequently occurring type of investment institution was that of investment house (26), followed by stockbrokers (14), insurance companies (12), banks (9) and two self-investing funds.[4] As expected, the pension funds predominate, being the most important type of fund under management for every type of institution except stockbrokers, for whom private clients were the most important type of fund. Very few of the funds were pooled, and so the performance of the fund managers could be scrutinised directly.

Table 1: Principal types of funds managed by investment institutions

	Type of investment institution						
Type of fund	*Insurance company*	*Stock-broker*	*Bank*	*Investment house*	*Self-investing*	*Total*	*Percent*
Pension fund	6	6	6	21	2	41	64.1%
Life assurance	7					7	10.9%
Unit trust			1			1	1.6%
Investment trust				2		2	3.1%
Private clients		7	2	3		12	18.8%
Charities		1				1	1.6%

There was a considerable range in the number and size of equity funds managed by interviewees, and a corresponding variation in the number of UK companies represented in a fund, ranging from 12 to 600 with a median and mode of 65. The typical fund had the following proportion of investments: gilts/bonds 11 per cent, UK equity 61 per cent, overseas equity 20 per cent, cash 6 per cent and property 2 per cent. There was a wide range of experience in the sample, with the shortest time as a fund manager being four years, the longest 47 years, with the average being 18 years. The exact role of the fund manager varied from institution to institution. All were involved in the selection of UK equities and some (27 per cent) had discretion on the proportion of the fund that was invested in other securities as well. Most commonly, the asset allocation decision was taken by a group within the manager's institution (62 per cent), while 11 per cent of the time the asset allocation decision was taken by the client. As indicated in Table 2, only 3 per cent of fund managers had the asset allocation specified by the trustee/client alone. In addition, most of the managers had complete discretion on what shares could be included in the UK equity part of the portfolio.

Table 2: Who makes the asset-allocation decision?

House decision	45.3%
House and fund manager together	4.7%
Fund manager alone	26.6%
Team of fund managers	12.5%
Fund manager and client together	7.8%
Trustee/client alone	3.1%

Performance appraisal systems

The incidence of performance monitoring was found to be high, with 94 per cent of the funds managed by interviewees reportedly subject to performance measurements on a quarterly, or more frequent, basis. Furthermore, 47 per cent of the fund managers reported that they were themselves performance appraised on a quarterly, or more frequent, basis. The most frequently occurring benchmark against which performance was appraised was that of the median fund, with a frequency of 60 per cent of respondents, followed by the all-share index, with a frequency of 44 per cent. Thirteen per cent of interviewees reported that they were not performance measured, 9 per cent claimed to be measured relative to other fund managers, and 5 per cent had other benchmarks such as the charities index.

A number of fund managers claimed to be measured against both the median fund performance and the all-share index. As can be seen from Table 4, those fund managers not measured against a benchmark occurred predominantly among private client fund managers, 30 per cent of whom claimed not to be performanced measured. The 13 per cent occurring among pension fund managers were drawn either from in-house funds or from organisations which had their roots in the mutual societies of the past, and had attempted to 'educate' pension fund trustees away from such benchmarking.

Table 3: Benchmarking for fund manager appraisal

	% of respondents
Median fund	60%
All-share index	44%
Peers	9%
Other	5%
None	13%

From Table 4 it can be seen that the median fund performance is the predominant benchmark for pension funds, with 71 per cent of pension fund managers measured against the median fund performance, while for private client funds it is the all-share index, with 70 per cent measured against it. Forty two per cent of pension fund managers were assessed against the all-share index, but over half of this group (26.3 per cent of the total sample of pension fund managers) were assessed against both benchmarks. Life funds showed a similar pattern, with 71.4 per cent assessed against the median fund performance, 42.8 per cent against the all-share index and 14.2 per cent against both. In contrast, only 20 per cent of private client fund managers were assessed against the median fund, 70 per cent against the all-share index, 20 per cent against both and 30 per cent not measured against any benchmark.

Table 4: Cross-tabulation of type of fund by benchmark (% frequency)

	All-share index	Median fund	Both	None
Pension funds	42.1%	71.0%	26.3%	13.1%
Life funds	42.8%	71.4%	14.2%	0
Private client funds	70.0%	20.0%	20.0%	30.0%

In order to partition the sample into groups according to benchmark, those respondents measured against both the median fund and the all-share index were eliminated from the sample. As can be seen from Table 5, the median fund still predominates as the relevant benchmark for pension funds (44.7 per cent), while for private clients it is still the all-share index (50 per cent).

Table 5: Benchmark by type of fund excluding joint all-share index and median fund performance benchmarks

	All-Share index	Median fund	None
Pension fund	15.7%	44.7%	13.1%
Life fund	28.5%	57.1%	0
Private client fund	50.0%	0	30.0%

In contrast to the importance of relative performance as indicated by the benchmarking employed, absolute levels of return were considered relatively unimportant (Table 6). However, a Kruskal Wallis one-way analysis of variance showed a significant difference (at the 10 per cent level) between respondent groups when analysed according to benchmark. Those expressing the view that absolute return was important were predominantly private client stockbrokers, for whom external performance measurement agencies are less relevant.

Table 6: Importance of absolute performance

No importance	26.6%
Slight importance	32.8%
Moderate importance	23.4%
Considerable importance	7.8%
Extreme importance	9.4%

Table 7: Importance of absolute performance by type of fund

	Pension fund	Life fund	Private client	$\chi 2$	Significance
Importance *	2.3	1.9	3.9		
Kruskal Wallis mean rank	29.33	23.43	40.35	5.6	0.06

(* Mean value: 1 = no importance; 5 = extreme importance)

The following comments from fund managers are indicative of the general feeling towards performance and the need to conform.

> *'For our business it [absolute performance] is not particularly important, which I always thought as rather odd. There is no doubt that CAPS and WM medians have become a sort of slave and all fund managers tend to be measured against them, and that is a problem, I think, for the industry.'*

> *'It doesn't matter what your absolute performance is. . . . What I have to do is ensure that this fund can act as a window for our sales force. It's got to be median or above, otherwise we can't sell it. We can't sell ourselves as decent fund managers. That's why it's got to be appraised against WM. Everybody recognises that method.'*

> *'The fact of the matter is, if you're in the top decile for CAPS, you get patted on the head by the client. If you are in the bottom decile, you'll probably be fired. So the temptation is to be in the 3rd to 7th and that means not deviating usually from the CAPS median. And because the CAPS median is what everybody else is doing, we're all chasing our own tail and there's a dangerous circularity in the whole thing.'*

> *'If your livelihood depends on the retention of funds and if those funds are being measured by WM every three months, and if you know that three or four bad quarterly performances are going to cost you your fund, then you tend to reduce and reduce and reduce your exposure to anything outside the Index.'*

Rewards received by fund managers

The importance of the rewards or penalties that the investment managers identified as being received are summarised in Table 8. It can be seen that while investment managers held an ambivalent view towards peer group status, senior management approval, promotion and salary, they held more well-defined views towards trustee approval, personal reputation (that is, in the labour market) and the feeling of doing a good job. The latter factor was ranked as the most important, with 86 per cent of respondents claiming it to be considerably to extremely important; followed by trustee approval, with 72 per cent feeling this to have considerable to extreme importance. As peer group status, senior management approval, promotion and salary are all related to standing in the firm, it can be expected that they would exhibit similar importance.

Similarly, the feeling of doing a good job will be related to trustee approval, as the investment manager is called to give account of the performance of the fund to the trustees, a task which can prove either enjoyable or painful. As one fund manager put it:

> *'Yes, it [meeting the trustees] is a very good discipline and it happens every quarter virtually with every fund, so you build a relationship and it is very important; and after all, that is what your job is, to keep them happy.'*

Table 8: Importance of motivating factors

	Percentage of respondent				
	None	Slight	Moderate	Considerable	Extreme
Peer group status	12.5	17.2	25.0	37.5	7.8
Senior management approval	15.6	9.4	29.7	31.3	14.1
Trustee approval	4.7	3.1	20.3	31.3	40.6
Promotion	20.3	17.2	26.6	21.9	14.1
Salary	17.2	15.6	25.0	26.6	15.6
Personal reputation	6.3	10.9	20.3	39.1	23.4
Feeling doing good job	1.6	0	12.5	34.4	51.6

A Kruskal Wallis analysis of variance (see Table 9) revealed a significant difference between private client fund managers (who held that they had a close relationship with their clients), pension fund managers (who report on a quarterly basis to the trustees) and the life fund managers, on the factors of trustee approval and salary. Trustee approval, as expected, was of lower importance to life fund managers (significant at the 10 per cent level), but salary was significantly more important (at the 5 per cent level)). Although no significant differences are disclosed (at the 10 per cent level) when analysed by benchmark (Table 10), trustee approval is of greater importance (significant at 12 per cent level) to those fund managers measured against the median fund performance, while the feeling of doing a good job is of least importance to these managers, and of greatest importance to those managers not measured against a benchmark.

The link between external performance monitoring, trustee pressure and motivation was spelled out by one fund manager in the following way:

> *'There is increasing pressure from most trustees. I have been in the industry for twenty years and it has changed. . . . Until about ten years ago the fund manager was working with the client together to achieve a common objective; and now . . . what has happened is the performance measurement surveys have turned fund management into a commodity, and the atmosphere is much more confrontational now. You go to a meeting at the end of the year and they look at the CAPS board and they say either well done, or they say this doesn't look very good; and it's much more like we are going in, as it were, to be marked at school than working in a partnership. . . . There is much more trustee pressure than there was.'*

Table 9: Importance of motivating factors: by type of fund

	Pension fund *	Life fund *	Private client *	Kruskal Wallis test $\chi 2$	significance
Motivator:					
Peer group status	3.1	3.4	3.0	0.36	0.83
Senior management approval	3.3	3.3	2.8	1.18	0.55
Trustee approval	4.2	2.9	4.1	8.71	0.01
Promotion	3.0	3.1	2.7	0.49	0.77
Salary	2.9	4.1	2.4	6.20	0.04
Personal reputation	3.6	4.0	3.5	0.80	0.66
Feeling doing good job	4.3	4.0	4.7	3.97	0.13

(* values shown are mean value of 5 point scale: 1=no importance; 5= extreme importance)

Table 10: Importance of motivating factors: by benchmark

	Median fund *	All-share fund *	None *	Kruskal Wallis test $\chi 2$	significance
Motivator:					
Peer group status	2.9	3.3	3.1	0.96	0.61
Senior management approval	3.3	3.6	2.5	3.14	0.20
Trustee approval	4.3	3.8	3.8	4.14	0.12
Promotion	3.0	3.0	2.5	0.83	0.65
Salary	3.0	3.4	2.6	1.63	0.44
Personal reputation	3.6	4.1	3.1	3.32	0.18
Feeling doing good job	4.2	4.4	4.8	3.29	0.19

(* values shown are mean value of 5 point scale: 1=no importance; 5= extreme importance)

Responses of fund managers to performance appraisal and reward

The way that the fund managers responded to a performance appraisal system based on their performance relative to a benchmark was to amend the normal risk/return trade-offs. In modern portfolio theory, the assumption is that investors will attempt to produce the portfolio which has the risk/return trade-off which gives the investor the highest utility. In this context, risk is measured in terms of the variance or standard deviation of the portfolio. Under the capital asset pricing model, risk is measured by the beta coefficient. In contrast, Tables 11 and 12 report the results of the interviews regarding the risk that fund managers considered to be important. From this, it can be seen that the absolute risk of a portfolio is of little importance. The most important risk is the failure to meet fund obligations in terms of asset and liability matching, considered important by 68 per cent of the investment managers interviewed. This was closely followed by commercial or business risk (that is, is the risk of relatively poor performance resulting in loss of the fund management contract), considered important by 45 per cent of the interviewees, while only 27 per cent considered the total variability of return to be important and 17 per cent considered beta of the portfolio to be important.

Table 11: Attitudes to risk by type of fund: analysis of variance

	Pension fund	Life assurance	Private client	% of total respondents	Kruskal Wallis test $\chi 2$	significance
Commercial risk:						
important	21	3	3	45%		
not important	20	4	9	55%	2.55	0.27
Asset/liability:						
important	25	7	9	68%		
not important	16	0	3	32%	4.44	0.10
Total variability:						
important	11	3	2	27%		
not important	30	4	10	73%	1.51	0.46
Beta of portfolio:						
important	8	1	1	17%		
not important	33	6	11	83%	0.85	0.65

The various forms of risk were explained by the managers as follows:

> *'There's two kinds of risk; there's investment risk, which is what the funds themselves bear, and there's business risk from [the fund management firm's] perspective, which is how much risk do we want to take with this client's fund, because doing badly is a lot worse than doing good is good.'*

> *'I can certainly say that no share has ever been bought on the basis of its beta or standard deviation. We only do it for interest and for the trustees' entertainment. Some trustees will occasionally ask what is the beta of my portfolio. So we say:* if you really want to know, it's 1!. . . *The performance risk against the benchmark is more of a risk for us.'*

When analysed according to the type of fund managed and according to the benchmark for appraisal, certain differences arose. All three types of fund manager groups (by type of fund managed) regarded asset liability matching as the most important measure of risk, although life fund managers attach significantly greater importance to it than do the other groups (significant at the 10 per cent level). No other risk measure (Table 11) exhibited a significant difference; consequently it may be concluded that the low importance attached to the beta coefficient by the interviewees was not a function of the type of fund under management, but a consensus view. However, commercial risk is seen to be of greater importance to managers of pension funds (51 per cent of this group) than to managers of life funds (43 per cent of this group) or private client funds (25 per cent of this group).

When the same risk attitudes were analysed against benchmarks (Table 12), the beta coefficient and total variability of return are again seen to be unimportant to all groups, while asset/liability matching is held by all groups to be important. However, a significant difference is displayed (at the 1 per cent level) for total variability of return, which was shown to be more important to median fund benchmarked managers than to either all-share benchmarked, or no benchmark funds. One explanation for this could lie in the desire of pension fund trustees (in view of their outflow commitments) to maintain steady income streams, or to avoid widely fluctuating performance. Of greater significance for this study is the result for commercial risk. While there was broad agreement across all three benchmark groups regarding the importance or otherwise of the other risk measures, the only group to consider commercial risk to be important was that subject to median fund benchmarking. This difference was statistically significant at the 10 per cent level.

Table 12: Attitudes to risk measures: analysis of variance by benchmark

	All-share index	Median fund	None	Kruskal Wallis test $\chi 2$	significance
Commercial risk:					
important	3	13	2		
not important	11	11	6	5.25	0.07
Asset/liability:					
important	9	19	6		
not important	5	5	2	1.54	0.46
Total variability:					
important	2	11	0		
not important	12	13	8	8.52	0.01
Beta of portfolio:					
important	2	5	0		
not important	12	19	8	2.11	0.34

In the words of one fund manager:

> *'If you are away from the average you run quite a risk.'*

And from the head of investment management of a merchant bank:

> *'The biggest risk we run is of getting our strategy wrong and producing a performance which is below average. If we perform above the median on a reasonably regular basis, we will retain it [the fund management contract]. Recently we had a slightly disappointing run of performance, so a number of our client relationships are rather sensitive.'*

6 Conclusions

The results of the interviews indicate that the performance evaluation system used to judge the work of fund managers had a constraining effect on their activities. The incentive to join the herd was strengthened by the fact that the herd were the benchmark. The risky position was to be different from the average.

For managers of funds subjected to performance monitoring relative to the median fund performance, the effect was seen to be a reluctance to pursue an investment strategy which could result in a performance which diverged significantly from the average. Performance at, or around, the median performance was considered to be the 'safe' strategy. This would not jeopardise the management contract with the fund trustees. Attempting to achieve 'top' performance, that is, in the top two deciles, would entail pursuit of an investment strategy different from the majority of pension fund managers. Such a strategy could be either successful and rewarded, or unsuccessful and punished. It is the fear of the consequences of pursuing a different and unsuccessful strategy which drives such investment managers to adopt the same approach.

Thus, within this performance monitoring context, risk is not viewed as the textbook measures of risk; nor is the absolute level of return considered important. After the overriding requirement that the fund assets generate sufficient income to meet fund liabilities (the pension payments), what matters to the investment manager is the level of performance relative to the benchmark. The possibility of under-performance is feared more than the potential for out-performance is welcomed. If performance matches the average, the fund manager is safe. It does not matter if the fund actually loses value as long as other comparator funds have suffered in the same way. To be different is to be risky. Thus, in order to reduce commercial risk to a minimum, such fund managers will adopt the same strategy as other fund managers who are measured against the same benchmark. In this scenario the variance (or standard deviation) of the portfolio, or the beta of the portfolio, become irrelevant.

Notes

1. Given two investments yielding the same return but with different estimates of risk, the risk-averse investor would chose the investment with the lowest estimate of risk.

2. Pension funds, insurance companies, investment trusts and unit trusts.

3. Of the two performance monitoring agencies for pension fund portfolios, World Markets claimed to cover 77 per cent of pension funds (mainly the larger funds) and Combined Actuarial Performance claimed to cover 46 per cent of pension funds (mainly the smaller funds). (1990 figures).

4. Pension funds managed internally by employees of the firm itself, rather than by an external manager.

References

Bar-Hillel, M. (1973), 'On the subjective probability of compound events', *Organisational Behaviour and Human Performance*, 9, pp. 396–406.

Bazerman, M.H. (1984), 'The relevance of Kahneman's and Tversky's concept of framing to organisational behaviour', *Journal of Management*, 10, pp. 333–343.

Blume, M.E. and Friend, I. (1973), 'A new look at the Capital Asset Pricing Model', *Journal of Finance*, vol 28, March, pp. 19–33.

Blume, M. and Friend, I. (1975), 'The asset structure of individual portfolios and some implications for utility functions', *Journal of Finance*, May.

Budescu, D.V. and Weiss, W. (1987), 'Reflection of transitive and intransitive preferences: a test of prospect theory', *Organizational Behaviour and Human Decision Processes*, 39, pp. 184–202.

Charkham, J. (1990), 'Are shares just commodities?', in *Creative Tension*, National Association of Pension Funds, London.

Coombs, C.H. (1975), 'Portfolio theory and the measurement of risk', in *Human Judgement and Decision Process*, Kaplan and Schwartz (eds), Academic Press, New York.

Eadie, D.M. (1987), 'The investment manager vanishes', *Money Magazine Forum*, December.

Eiser, J.R. and Van der Pligt, J. (1988), *Attitudes and Decisions*, Routledge, London.

Ellsberg, D. (1961), 'Risk, ambiguity and the savage axioms', *Quarterly Journal of Economics*, 75, pp. 643–69.

Fama, E.F. and French, K.R. (1992), 'The cross-section of expected stock returns', *Journal of Finance*, 47, June.

Fiegenbaum, A. and Thomas, H. (1988), 'Attitudes toward risk and the risk–return paradox: prospect theory explanations', *Academy of Management Journal*, 31, 1.

Fishburn, P.C. and Kochenberger, G.A. (1979), 'Two-piece Von Neumann-Morgenstern utility functions', *Decision Sciences*, 10,4.

Gooding, A.E. (1979), 'Perceived risk and capital asset pricing', *Journal of Finance*, Vol. 33, 5, Dec, pp. 1401–1421.

Hershey, J.C. and Schoemaker, P.J.H. (1980), 'Risk taking and problem context in the domain of losses – an expected utility analysis', *Journal of Risk Insurance*, 47,1.

Kahneman, D. and Tversky, A. (1979), 'Prospect theory: an analysis of decision under risk', *Econometrica*, 47,2.

Kahneman, D. and Tversky, A. (1986), 'Rational choice and the framing of decisions', *Journal of Business*, 59, 4, 2.

Kameda, T. and Davis, J.H. (1990), 'The function of the reference point in individual and group risk decision making', *Organisational Behaviour and Human Perspectives*, 46, pp. 55–76.

Kunreuther, H., and Slovic, P. (1978), 'Economics, psychology and protective behaviour', *American Economic Review*, 68,2.

Laing, H. (1990), 'The balance of responsibilities', in *Creative Tension*, National Association of Pension Funds, London.

Lawler, E.E. (1969), 'Job design and employee motivation', *Personnel Psychology*, 22, pp. 426–35.

Lazar, D. (1990), *Markets and Ideology in the City of London*, Macmillan, Basingstoke.

Lever, C. (1989), 'Don't shoot the performance measurer', *Pensions Management*, December.

Markowitz, H.M. (1952), 'Portfolio selection', *Journal of Finance*, 7, March, pp. 77–91.

Markowitz, H.M. (1959), *Portfolio Selection: Efficient Diversification of Investments*, John Wiley, New York

Mintzberg, H. (1975), *The Nature of Managerial Work*, Harper/Row, New York.

Mosteller, F. and Nogee, P. (1951), 'An experimental measurement of utility', *Journal of Political Economy*, 59, 5, pp. 371–404.

Phillips & Drew (1990), *Pension Fund Indicators*, Phillips & Drew Fund Management Ltd, London.

Plastow, D. (1990), 'Corporate strategy and the institutional shareholder', in *Creative Tension*, National Association of Pension Funds, London.

Schoemaker, P.J.H. and Kunreuther, H.C. (1979), 'An experimental study of insurance decisions', *Journal of Risk Insurance*, 46,4.

Simon, H.A. (1955), 'A behavioural model of rational choice', *Quarterly Journal of Economics*, 69, pp. 99–118.

Slovic et al (1977), 'Preference for insuring against probably small losses: insurance implications', *Journal of Risk Insurance*, 44,2.

Thomas, W.A. (1989), *The Securities Market*, Philip Allan, Hemel Hempstead.

Tversky, A. (1969), 'Intransitivity of preferences', *Psychology Review*, 76, 1, pp. 31–48.

Performance Measurement in Charities

David Wise
(South Bank University)

Performance Measurement in Charities

Introduction

> *'An individual who intends only his own gain is led by an invisible hand to promote an end which was no part of his intention. Nor is it always the worse for the society that it was no part of it. By pursuing his own interest he frequently promotes that of the society more effectually than when he really intends to promote it. I have never known much good done by those who affected to trade for the public good.'*
>
> *Adam Smith,* The Wealth of Nations, *1776*
>
> *quoted by Milton Friedman,* Free to Choose, *Pelican Books, 1980*

It is common when questioning the efficiency of charities to hear comments such as:

- the value of charity work cannot be expressed in money terms;
- all charities are different and cannot be compared;
- expenditure ratios are meaningless in charities;
- return on investment does not apply to the non-profit sector;

and so on.

While recognising some truth in all these statements, it seems to me to be abrogating our responsibility as managers to accept them entirely. It is true that there are many difficulties in assessing performance in the not-for-profit sector. But in this paper I would like to explore approaches to measuring performance – since without measurement there can be no objective management of results nor any real concept of improving performance.

This paper looks first at some theoretical frameworks for positioning performance measurement in organisations, before going on to explore why performance measurement in charities is more difficult and more demanding than in commercial enterprises.

The paper then draws on the public sector concept of value for money and the three Es to provide a model for reviewing performance in charities, and looks at some empirical evidence of relationships between size and efficiency before suggesting some avenues for improving performance measurement in charities.

Performance and control

Charities, like any other organisation, have inputs which are processed in some way to provide outputs. Controlling the performance of the organisation has been said to depend on the availability of output measures and knowledge of the transformation process (*Ouchi*, 1977). This dependence is shown in Figure 1.

Figure 1: Control choices

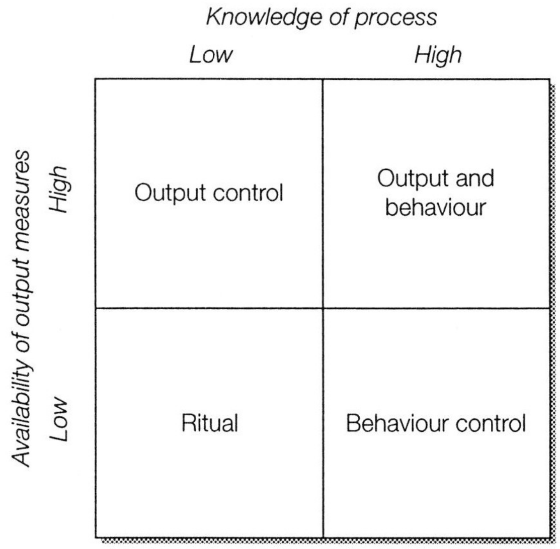

In my experience, many charities have tended to have a poor method for recording and controlling output measurement even though they may understand the processes – tending to place charities in the south-east corner of this matrix. But, of course, charities vary widely.

Where would you place a charity which you are acquainted with on this matrix? In the case of religious activities, where there is no scientific measurement of process or outputs, faith and ritual are important control mechanisms. Commercial businesses expect to control both behaviour (and associated costs) and outputs (in the form of sales income) in seeking to maximise profitability.

In terms of managing an organisation and taking decisions on courses of action to control its performance, management must seek to clarify, as part of the planning process, the objectives of the operations and the consequences of the alternative actions available. This may be set out as another matrix – see Figure 2 (*Open University*, 1993).

Figure 2: Control processes

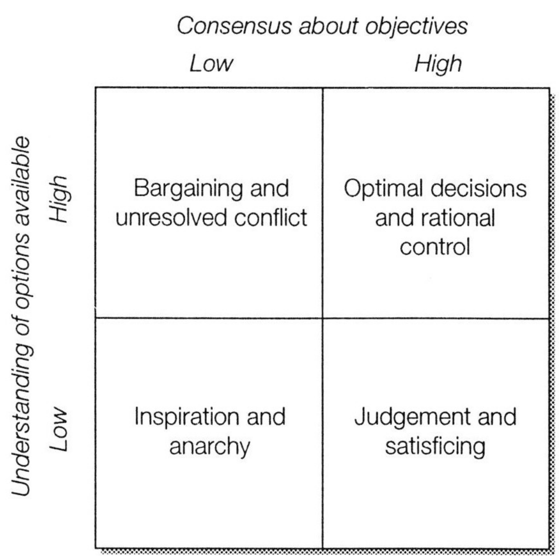

My view is that in recent years many charities have improved their corporate planning and, as a result, have achieved greater consensus about objectives. Understanding of options in terms of quantified costs and benefits is often a difficulty, however, which again tends to push charities towards the south-east segment of the matrix.

In business organisations, where profit optimisation is an influence towards goal congruence, it may be easier to establish consistent aims and to evaluate alternative strategies. In a charity, which does not have so clear a unifying goal of profitability, the treasurer and financial director have to work harder to provide a framework for optimal decision-making and rational control.

Differences between charities and private/public sector

> *One of the most basic differences between non-profit organisations and businesses is that the typical non-profit has so many more relationships that are vitally important. In all but the very biggest businesses, the key relationships are fewer – employees, customers, and owners, and that's all. Every non-profit organisation has a multitude of constituencies and has to work out the relationship with each of them.*
>
> *Peter Drucker,* Managing the Non-profit Organisation, *Oxford, 1990 as quoted by Ian Bruce,* Charity Talks on Successful Development, *City University Business School, 1993.*

The question is often posed, especially by those outside the charity sector, as to why charities require special treatment at all and why they should be subject to requirements of accountability in some respects more onerous than those applied to commercial business under the Companies Acts. Those concerned in charitable work also question the increasing burdens of accountability placed on trustees and managers by the recent changes in legislation.

It is possible to respond to such questions empirically by pointing to the major charity frauds and financial scandals which appear in the press from time to time, and the anecdotal evidence of more widespread minor financial irregularities in very small local voluntary bodies.

In theory, too, it can be argued that shareholders in commercial businesses expect to balance the conflicts of risk and return whenever they invest their money in a business. We may properly expect such shareholders to exercise due caution with regard to their own money, and they are assisted in their risk-taking by a large infrastructure of corporate and financial analysts, investment advisers and city commentators. The donors who contribute to charities are usually less well equipped to take decisions on costs and benefits, while the beneficiaries of charitable activities are hardly ever in a position to judge whether they receive value for money.

Moreover, the structure of the market in which commercial businesses operate is one which regulates itself in economic terms through two basic feedback mechanisms. On a strategic level a commercial business relies on external investors to provide finance for the firm. Unless those investors receive a satisfactory return on their investment, then the firm will be unlikely to gain access to further finance. On a tactical level, a commercial business must sell products. Unless it does so it will not make a profit and will not be able to sustain a return to its investors.

Neither of the two control mechanisms referred to above apply to the not-for-profit sector. However, the spread of contractual arrangements between government and voluntary bodies, whereby the amount of government grant is tied to delivery of services, does seek to provide a feedback loop similar to the price mechanism. This does, of course, turn such charities into mere agents of the state, as indeed is recommended by *Knight* (1993).

A commercial business links its corporate financing to the continued operation of its revenue earning activities by investment in fixed and intangible assets which support and sustain those activities. A charity tends, if it is able to, to seek continuity and stability of income by maintaining a reserve of charitable funds as investments to provide a source of support for future funding levels. These differences are shown in Figures 3a and 3b.

Figure 3a: Movement of funds in a business

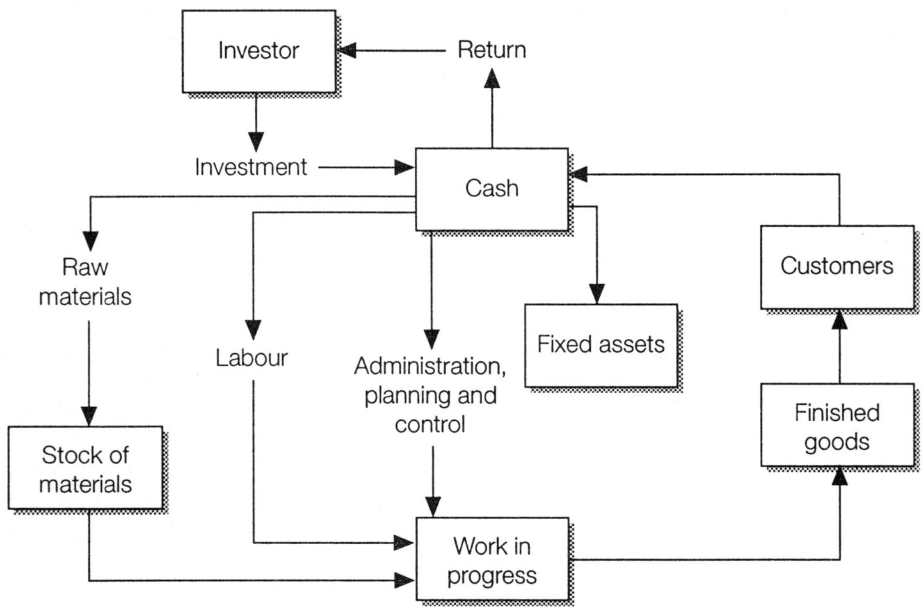

Figure 3b: Movement of funds in a charity

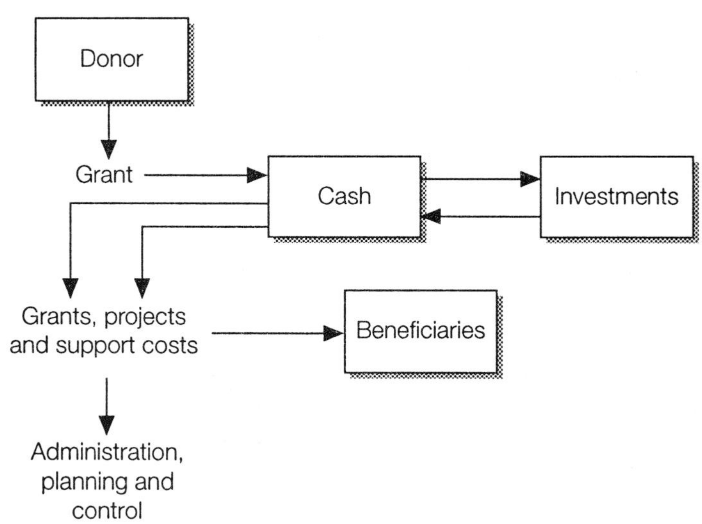

Investment appraisal is a key concern in corporate finance; investment management and reserve levels are major strategic concerns for city finance directors. The importance of investment management is illustrated by the analysis of the largest charities' balance sheets shown in Table 1 (based on the 2,071 largest charities on the Hemmington Scott 1992 charities database):

Table 1: Charity balance sheet

	1992		1991	
	£m	%	£m	%
Fixed assets	5,586	22	5,622	24
Investments	17,410	70	15,952	67
Net current assets	–237	–1	–442	–2
Liquid assets	2,136	9	2,538	11
Total funds	24,895	100	23,669	100

The absence of the investment reward motive, and the fact that charities are unable to earn profits, means that the principal performance measures which apply to business undertakings cannot be used in most charitable undertakings. Charities have to try to develop other measures of efficiency and effectiveness. In this respect the best charities are well ahead of the business community, which has generally been slower to recognise the need to report on non-financial performance indicators.

The competitive market, like the law of the jungle, ensures by the rough justice of the survival of the fittest that only the efficient business survives in the long run. The commercial means of weeding out uncompetitive businesses by investor pressure, divestment, merger, acquisition or ultimately liquidation, do not naturally control the efficiency of charities – hence the need for the Charities Commission.

During the recent recession, the number of companies going out of business exceeded the numbers of new companies formed, as financially marginal businesses became unable to compete. Compare this with the birth and death of charities. In 1992 the Commission began a data cleaning exercise aimed in part at identifying charities which had ceased to operate or been wound up, but it still registered 4,691 charities (compared with 4,042 in 1991) and removed only 4,546 (1,168 in 1991). New charities are being registered at the rate of two in every working hour (even the Lloyd's of London Names Support Fund applied to be a charity for the relief of poverty!). However, it is difficult to weed out those who should no longer qualify.

Overall, the task of measuring performance in the voluntary sector, and the financial issues relating to charities, some of which are referred to above, require much more sensitive analysis than is required in the commercial world.

Analysing value for money performance

There are two fools in every market; the one who pays too much and the one who pays too little.
Old Russian proverb

If you pay too much you may lose some money. If you pay too little you may lose everything.
Sign in jeweller's window

The complex concept of how to evaluate value for money can be simplified by breaking it down into three aspects: economy, efficiency and effectiveness, where economy implies minimal expenditure consistent with the aims (value analysis in engineering terminology), efficiency implies the relationship of outputs to inputs (equivalent to productivity), and effectiveness implies the relationship between outputs and aims. These factors – the three Es – can be related to each other as Figure 4 illustrates.

Figure 4: Value for money

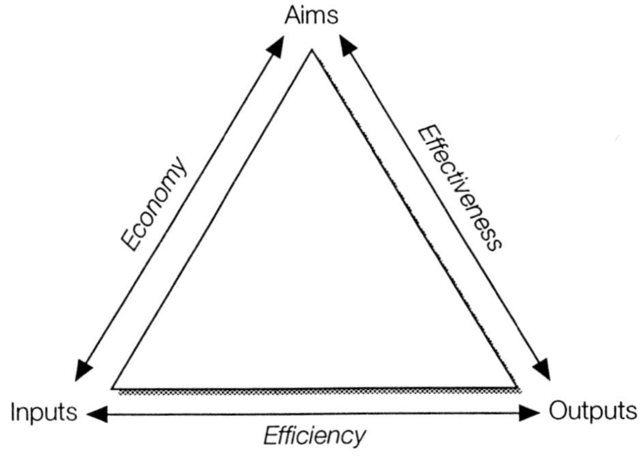

In a commercial business the main element is that of efficiency; the difference between cost inputs and revenue outputs, which represents profit and which is itself a principal aim. However, public services, even if required to break even or to earn a return on capital, usually have to place emphasis on effectiveness above efficiency, since they frequently serve national economic or social ends, whose results are likely to take precedence over mere financial surplus. The efficiency of airport operations is important, but the public will forgive some lack of efficiency if operations are effective in preventing air collisions and terrorist activities, for example. Even in the private sector the profit motive of shareholders is modified increasingly by the interests of the community at large, giving rise to an alternative three Es: ethics, environment and equity.

The nature of the charities sector is also likely to impact unfavourably on the search for value for money. *Milton Friedman* classifies spending under four cases, depending on whether you are spending your own money or someone else's, and whether you are spending for your own benefit or for the benefit of someone else. If you spend your own money on yourself you are concerned with economy, efficiency and effectiveness. If you are spending your own money on someone else, as when buying a present, you are concerned with economy but less with efficiency. If you are spending someone else's money on yourself, as with an expense account lunch, you don't worry too much about economy but you are going to ensure effectiveness and to get your money's worth. If you are spending someone else's money on someone else then you have no direct motivation to seek economy, efficiency or effectiveness.

Trustees of charities are, of course, in the latter position. As *Friedman* (1980) says of bureaucrats in relation to state welfare state programmes, they

> *'spend someone else's money on someone else. Only human kindness, not the much stronger and more dependable spur of self-interest, assures that they will spend the money in the way most beneficial to the recipients. Hence the wastefulness and ineffectiveness of the spending.'*

Trustees have legal duties and no doubt most trustees act responsibly, but they have no business motivation to achieve value for money. Indeed, they are prohibited generally from receiving any financial reward for carrying out their duties as trustees, even if they perform exceptionally well. Failures in providing value for money frequently arise, and spectacular failures are reported in the press from time to time. For these reasons, charities need to put disciplines and systems in place to safeguard the interests of the beneficiaries, who can usually exert little power over the way money is spent by charities.

Efficiency in charities

> *'Nobody ever believes that his own performance is measurable. Each of us discerns in ourselves intangible, even undemonstrable, and certainly unquantifiable virtues. What we do, we feel, is so much more than any accountant could ever reduce to a set of figures.'*
>
> *Matthew Paris,* The Times, *25 June 1994*

The measurement of efficiency implies a measure of the relationship between inputs of resources and the value of outputs. This is a common indicator for commercial organisations, where inputs can be expressed as costs or as capital employed and outputs can be expressed as sales or profits, for example.

In non-profit-based organisations these figures are not available in the sense in which they are found in businesses. However, the purpose of charitable bodies is to act as a channel for transferring resources from the donors to the beneficiaries or the charitable objects of the charity. Efficiency in this sense of input/output measurement can be indicated from the accounts of charities. The resources coming into the charity are readily identifiable from the accounts, though the amount of expenditure regarded as benefiting the beneficiaries is less easily defined. Expenditure by way of grants is clearly of direct benefit to beneficiaries. In addition, it may be postulated that expenditure on service provision gives a benefit to the beneficiary, whereas administration costs will reduce the amount available for the purposes of the charity.

My early experience in carrying out investigations in charities led me to feel that there are too many charities operating in the same areas of activity (*Wise*, 1989). From a marketing or needs identification point of view, small local operations are likely to be most desirable. But from a financial point of view the proliferation of charities is likely to be wasteful of resources, since it may be expected that administrative costs will be proportionately less in larger charities which can benefit from economies of scale.

To test this expectation, a sample was taken from the *Henderson Top 2000 Charities Guide 1994* covering the 25 largest, the 25 smallest, and 25 half way through the list. The results are shown in Table 2, which compares the three size groups.

As can be seen from Table 2, the larger charities appear to be more efficient. Benefits to beneficiaries measured by the sum of grants paid plus costs of service provision accounted for 84 per cent of the income of large charities, 68 per cent in the case of medium-sized charities, and only 61 per cent of small charities. Administration costs on the other hand account for under 9 per cent of large charities' income, 14 per cent of medium charities' and over 23 per cent of the small charities' income.

There are large differences between charities, which makes further research desirable. The figures themselves are open to further analysis and, of course, the value of services to beneficiaries is greatly understated because the accounts do not include the value of volunteer labour inputs and outputs. However, the analysis so far undertaken does suggest that it would be in the interests of beneficiaries that smaller charities should be seeking mergers, alliances, or other ways to combine and share administrative functions.

Effectiveness in charities

> *'If people did not give money to beggars, beggars would not ask for it. They would find some other source of income. Besides, begging is efficient charity, a benefit in cash not in kind. Asking for money on the street is one-stop welfare at the point of delivery. Money is demanded only because it is given. The way to end begging is to make giving an offence – and the public would not stand for that.'*
>
> *'Proposal that beggars belief', Simon Jenkins,* The Times, *1 June 1994.*

The measurement of effectiveness is even more problematical than efficiency, since there can be no common measure for comparing charities with differing aims and objectives.

For individual charities it is important that objectives are clearly defied in the planning process. Clarity of objectives stems from:

- a *vision* of where we want to be – possibly expressed in a mission statement or statement of purpose;
- an analysis of where we are, our present course of direction, and our *strengths and weaknesses;*
- an assessment of needs and an evaluation of *opportunities and threats;*
- consideration of the gap between the present and the desired position;
- formulation of alternative ways to exploit strengths and opportunities and to overcome threats and weaknesses;
- identification of *key performance areas* or *critical success factors.*

The measurement of effectiveness is therefore a final stage in the planning and control cycle which runs from long term to short term and from the general to the specific. Effectiveness requires:

- *Mission* – overall vision, mission of organisation, key themes.
- *Measures* – measures of success.
- *Means* – strategies, action steps, budgets.

Table 2: Large, medium and small charities in the Henderson Top 2000 charities

No. of charities	25		25		25		75	
	large		med.		small		total	
	£m	%	£m	%	£m	%	£m	%
Value of sample								
Total income	2524	100.0	34.9	100.0	13.16	100.0	2572	100.0
of which public grants, fee, etc.	901	35.7	8.8	25.1	1.15	8.7	911	35.4
Expenditure								
Grants made	954	37.8	5.1	14.6	4.55	34.6	964	37.5
Service provision	1284	50.9	18.6	53.3	3.41	25.9	1306	50.8
	2238	88.7	23.7	67.9	7.96	60.4	2269	88.2
Publications	26	1.0	0.4	1.1	0.13	1.0	27	1.0
Administration	268	10.6	5.0	14.5	3.06	23.2	276	10.7
Publicity and fund-raising	71	2.8	0.2	0.6	0.59	4.5	72	2.8
Other and exceptional	–131	–5.2	2.1	6.0	–0.07	–0.5	–129	-5.0
Total expenditure	2472	97.9	31.4	90.1	11.67	88.7	2515	97.8
Mean percentages								
Total income		100.0		100.0		100.0		100.0
of which public grants, fees, etc.		38.1		25.1		8.8		24.0
Expenditure								
Grants made		32.0		14.6		34.6		27.1
Service provision		52.3		53.4		25.9		43.9
		84.4		68.0		60.5		71.0
Publications		1.6		1.1		1.0		1.2
Administration		8.7		14.4		23.2		15.5
Publicity and fund-raising		4.2		0.6		4.5		3.1
Other and exceptional		–0.6		6.0		–0.5		1.6
Total expenditure		98.3		90.1		88.7		92.4

Non-financial performance measures

> *'To most people the concept of making a profit or having a surplus arising from sick people is distasteful. Yet almost everyone accepts that the only way to provide better treatment for patients out of finite sums available is to improve the use of those resources. . . . The problem is how to combine caring for health and life, which are beyond price, with the practical fact that if the cost per effectively treated patient is reduced, more patients can be treated.'*
>
> Return on Capital Employed Techniques in the NHS,
> *Chartered Institute of Management Accountants, 1994.*

For charities above all other organisations, non-financial measures are likely to be as important if not more important than financial measures. Information is best communicated through a combination of financial and non-financial measures. This is increasingly recognised even in the corporate sector, partly because of the increasing trend towards leaner middle management with greater delegation, and the move away from control-oriented, vertical functional structures to process-focused, multi-functional, faster and flatter team-based structures.

Meyer (1994) has four guiding principles which seem appropriate to the charity sector:

- The overarching purpose of a management system should be to help a team, rather than top managers, gauge its progress. It should primarily be a tool for telling the team when it must take corrective action.
- A truly empowered team must play the lead role in designing its own management system (though the resulting measurement system must be consistent with the overall strategy).
- Because a team is responsible for a value-delivery process it must create measures to track that process. Process measures should be used in conjunction with traditional functional measures.
- A team should adopt only a handful of measures – 15 is probably too many.

A further difficulty in measurement stems from the fact that there is rarely a close relationship between outputs which can usually be easily measured, outcomes which are less easily measured, and the strategic aims of the charity. For example, a charity with the main aim of improving educational standards in a third world country found that education was disrupted by the need of women to trek many miles in the dry season in search of water. Drilling wells became an objective to prevent absences so that schooling provision could be made effective. In the action plans of the charity, drilling wells was the output measure of tactical progress. The assumed connection with the strategic aim of greater school attendance could only be measured in the longer term and in the knowledge that there are other factors at work. Finally, improved educational standards which are assumed to follow from better school attendance are unlikely to be demonstrable until many years after the drilling of the wells.

This means that performance measurement systems need to be implemented at a number of levels, generating operational short-term measures and less frequent strategic long-term measures. Both outputs/outcomes and inputs need to be related to the main objectives of the charity.

Suggestions for the future

There are difficulties in measuring performance in charities and in motivating managers/trustees to make the efforts required to measure performance. Below are some suggestions for implementing procedures designed to introduce better performance measurement criteria:

- Charities significant to the national economy should be subject to VFM audit by the NAO or Audit Commission.

- Charity Commission should have power to require mergers when in the interests of beneficiaries of both charities.

- Charities should report:
  - how beneficiaries are defined;
  - how benefits (outputs) are measured;
  - how outputs relate to beneficial outcomes;
  - how trustees have assessed outcomes and resource allocation by charitable objectives (cf. government Resource Accounting Green Paper)
  - number and frequency of trustees' meeting (cf. Cadbury Corporate Governance Report).

- A Charities Charter should be promoted to ensure that beneficiaries understand complaints procedures and entitlements.

- More public resources should be provided:
  - to educate trustees, especially in performance measurement techniques, and to encourage best practice benchmarking
  - to improve management accounting and costing methods in charities.

References

Friedman, M (1988), *Free to Choose*, Penguin.

Knight, B (1993), *Voluntary Action in the 1990s*, Home Office.

Meyer, C (1994), *Harvard Business Review*, May–June.

Open University (1993), *Performance Measurement and Evaluation* (B889, Unit 2).

Ouchi, W. G. (1977), 'The relationship between organisational structure and organisational control', *Administrative Science Quarterly*, March.

Wise, D (1989), 'Maximising value from volunteers', *Management Accounting*, Feb.

Data Envelopment Analysis: A Tool for Management Accountants?

Valerie Belton and Derek Crowe
(University of Strathclyde)

Data Envelopment Analysis: A Tool for Management Accountants?

1 *Introduction*

This paper considers the potential for data envelopment analysis (DEA) as a tool for performance measurement in the service sector. This is illustrated through its use to evaluate the performance of branches of a UK clearing bank.

Many organisations in the service sector offer their services through multiple outlets: for example, branches of a bank, building society, estate agency, travel agency, or individual hotels in a chain. In each of these examples all outlets are offering the same service, or mix of services, to their customers. However, the outlets do not all operate at the same level, they do not utilise precisely the same resources, nor do they operate in exactly the same environment. DEA seeks to take account of all these factors in identifying which of these decision-making units (DMUs) are performing inefficiently in comparison with the others.

The approach was initially proposed some thirty years ago, but has relatively recently attracted the attention of both researchers and management practitioners (see, for example, *Norman and Stoker*, 1991). The underlying concept is an attractive one; the approach takes account of multiple inputs and multiple outputs in assessing the relative efficiency of units performing a similar task. In doing so it allows each unit total flexibility in determining the emphasis to be placed on each input and output, thus giving it the best opportunity to appear efficient.

There are now numerous accounts of the use of DEA in organisations, and a number of management consultancies are promoting the approach. It has been applied previously to the evaluation of bank branches in a number of organisations, as described by *Sherman and Gold* (1985), *Vassiloglou and Giokas* (1991), *Pastor* (1993) and *Drake and Howcroft* (1994). Each of these articles indicates a desire for a more broadly based assessment of performance than that offered by simple financial ratios.

This study investigated the application of DEA to evaluate the performance of branches of one of the UK clearing banks. Almost 60 branches, located within a recognised geographical region incorporating a major city, a number of towns and rural villages, were considered. The development of the DEA model used in the analysis, including the identification of relevant inputs and outputs, is described. Illustration of how these results can be used to set targets for inefficient branches are presented, and the efficiency measures generated by DEA are compared with cost/income ratios. The views of bank staff on the potential use of DEA are discussed.

Previous experience with applying DEA (*Belton and Vickers*, 1993) identified a number of limitations, in particular the 'black-box' nature of the approach, which reduces the likelihood of analyses being understood and accepted by managers. *Belton* (1992) suggested a re-interpretation of the formulation and the development of a visual interactive system as a way of facilitating understanding of the approach. Similar feedback was received from managers involved in this study. The revised approach is illustrated using some of the data from the case study. The experience and suggestions of others for suitable methods of visualising the results of a DEA analysis are also considered.

To investigate awareness of DEA among management accountants, a survey of CIMA members working in the financial sector was carried out. The findings of this survey are briefly reported.

Finally, we reflect on the implications of this study for the management accounting profession, and on fruitful areas for further research and development.

2 *Data envelopment analysis*

2.1 *The method*

DEA is an analytical technique which is used to evaluate the efficiency of outlets, or branches, of an organisation; these are generally referred to as decision-making units (DMUs), or simply units. The units utilise similar resources, referred to as inputs, to generate similar outputs. However, they operate at different levels, each unit producing a particular combination of outputs using its own mix of inputs. DEA compares each unit's use of its inputs and production of its outputs with all the other units in the dataset. It identifies those units which are operating relatively efficiently and those which are not. A unit which is efficient has a rating of 100 per cent and those which are inefficient have ratings of less than 100 per cent. An inefficient unit is one which should be able to produce its current level of outputs with fewer inputs, or generate a higher level of outputs given the same inputs, when compared with the actual achieved performance of other units in the dataset. An outline of the DEA model is given in the appendix.

The implementation of a DEA analysis involves:

- identifying the inputs and outputs of the function performed by the DMUs;
- identifying measures for the inputs and outputs;
- collecting data on the inputs and outputs;
- solving the DEA linear programming model;
- interpreting the solution.

The output from a DEA model provides:

- efficiency ratings for all DMUs in the dataset;
- for each inefficient DMU, the set of efficient DMUs against which it should be compared;
- information about how much emphasis has been placed on each input and output in calculating each DMU's efficiency rating;
- a set of target input or output values that an inefficient DMU would need to reach to achieve an efficiency rating of 100 per cent.

2.2 *Origins of DEA*

The concepts of DEA date back some 30 years to *Farrell* (1957). However, the current interest seems to have been initiated by *Charnes, Cooper and Rhodes* (1978), who proposed DEA as a way of measuring performance in non-profit and public sector organisations, the success of which cannot be measured by a single bottom-line figure such as profit.

Interest in the approach has extended beyond the public sector to commercial organisations where, traditionally, financial ratios have been used as a way of measuring a unit's performance. However, one of the limitations of such ratios is that only two dimensions of activity, represented by the numerator and denominator, can be examined in any one indicator. DMUs may do well on some ratios used to measure performance but not so well on others, making it difficult to summarise the overall performance of the DMUs in question. DEA, which takes into account multiple inputs and outputs in determining an efficiency measure for each unit, is a potential way of overcoming this limitation.

The application of DEA outside the public sector is, however, still at an early stage of development. One aim of this investigation is to compare the measurement of the efficiency of units using DEA with that obtained using the standard financial ratios, in order to investigate whether DEA adds value to the ratio analysis.

3 *Applications of DEA*

Since DEA was put forward by *Charnes, Cooper and Rhodes* in 1978, a large number of papers have been published on this technique. *Seiford* (1990) has complied a bibliography of these papers, which contains 400 references for the period 1978–90.

Most of the published papers are concerned with developing and enhancing the theoretical basis of the original *Charnes, Cooper and Rhodes* (1978) work. However, there are a number of papers reporting studies into the use of DEA to measure performance in practice. Most of these concern public sector organisations, for example, *Tomkins and Green* (1988) used DEA to assess the efficiency of UK university departments of accounting, *Thanassoulis, Dyson and Foster* (1987) assessed the rates departments of local authorities and *Miliotis* (1992) evaluated electricity distribution districts in Greece.

There have, however, been several reported applications of the use of DEA to assess the efficiency of the branches of banks. *Sherman and Gold* (1985), in their study of a US savings bank, found that DEA appeared to provide insights about bank branch performance not available from other performance measures, which are largely oriented towards profitability assessment. *Vassiloglou and Giokas* (1990) carried out a similar study applying DEA to the branches of the Commercial Bank of Greece. *Parkan* (1987) used DEA to compare the efficiency of 35 branches of a major Canadian chartered bank. He found that DEA provided a very useful first step towards developing relative efficiency measures for bank branches. *Oral, Kettani and Yolalan* (1992) used DEA to assess both the productivity and profitability of a bank's branches. They found that using DEA both complemented the traditional financial ratios and was also a useful bank management tool for reallocating resources between the branches. *Berg, Forsund and Jansen* (1991) applied DEA to measure the efficiency of a sample of 107 Norwegian banks and showed that the choice of output measures can have a major effect on the efficiency scores generated by the resulting DEA model.

The authors of these studies of DEA in banking have adopted different approaches to measuring the output of banks. *Colwell and Davis* (1992) conducted a survey of the empirical literature on productivity in banking and of the concepts used to measure bank output. They found that both output and productivity remain difficult to assess theoretically and are even harder to measure. There is fundamental disagreement over the nature of bank output, with a number of different approaches being used to measure it. Most of the studies measure bank output in one of two ways. They either consider the number of different categories of accounts or the volume of transactions carried out on them as the outputs. The other approach used is to consider banks as intermediators of financial services, and view the revenue generated on the stock of deposits as the bank's main output.

4 *Bank case study*

4.1 *Data availability*

The application of DEA to the measurement of performance in a financial services organisation is illustrated by using data supplied by a UK bank. This study focuses upon measuring the efficiency of a subset of the bank's branches, namely all those branches of the bank which are in a particular geographical area. The bank provided data relating to these branches for the years

1989/90 and 1991/92. This enabled DEA models to be constructed for two different years. In order to preserve the confidentiality of the bank's data, the data was scaled by the bank, and the branches concerned are referred to by a number rather than their name.

A project to develop a comprehensive new branch database was nearing completion at the time this study began, and it was envisaged that this database would be the source of information for the study. However, it was not available as early as anticipated; thus the initial study used data for the financial year 1989/90 which had been complied for an internal study of branch performance. This paper will focus upon the results obtained from using the 1989/90 dataset, which contained information relating to 58 branches, to illustrate the application of DEA.

Previous studies have taken different approaches to measuring branch output and productivity. The model which could be adopted in this study was restricted by the data available. It was not possible to construct a DEA model using as outputs the number of transactions processed by branches on their accounts, as data relating to this was not available.

Before carrying out the analysis a number of decisions needed to be taken about the detail of the model to be adopted. The original DEA formulation, developed by *Charnes, Cooper and Rhodes* (1978), assumes that the performance of DMUs shows constant returns to scale. This assumption was tested by plotting total income against total cost for the bank branches considered. The data points were evenly distributed above and below the line which, suggests that the assumption of constant returns to scale was a reasonable one.

If there had been an indication that the DMUs' performance was subject to variable returns to scale, a situation in which an increase in inputs does not result in a proportionate increase in outputs, then an alternative formulation of the DEA model could have been used. *Banker, Charnes and Cooper* (1984) have developed a DEA model which allows for variable returns to scale.

The DEA model used can address either of two questions, namely: 'Given the level of business that the branch conducts, how much could its inputs have been reduced by while maintaining that level of business?' (input minimisation) or 'Given the level of inputs used by the branch, how much output should it have achieved?' (output maximisation).

To facilitate interpretation of the results of an analysis, the output maximisation model would require an awareness of whether the market potential existed to allow the target outputs generated by the model to be achieved. Information regarding the market potential for each branch was not available, so the evaluation was carried out from a standpoint of input minimisation.

4.2 *Determining inputs and outputs*

The selection of relevant inputs and outputs is critical to the success of a DEA efficiency assessment. *Sherman* (1984) argues that

> *'When relevant outputs and inputs are excluded because they were overlooked, too difficult to measure, or unmeasurable, the DEA results can be biased and possibly misleading.'*

However, unlike in econometric model building where variables are eliminated from consideration by using hypothesis tests, there is no standard method for choosing input and output variables in a DEA model. Various suggestions have been made in the literature as to how to select the 'most relevant' variables for a particular set of DMUs. *Ganley and Cubbin* (1992) point out, however, and we would agree, that the selection of appropriate inputs and outputs remains essentially a subjective exercise which at best is based on expert opinion. They suggest that the credibility of DEA models would be increased if more formal, less disputable selection criteria were developed.

There is concern that without a formal method of variable selection it will be easier for DMUs to manipulate their efficiency score. DMUs can be expected to argue for the inclusion in the model of those variables which make them appear as efficient as possible. DMUs may argue for the maximum number of variables to be included in the model, as this will increase the likelihood that a DMU will be found to be efficient. If the number of DMUs is small relative to the number of input and output measures used, then there is greater opportunity for each unit to appear efficient, and it is, perhaps, less likely that useful insights will arise.

To help identify those factors which were most significant in their influence on branch performance we used an approach suggested by *Norman and Stoker* (1991), referred to as the stepwise approach. The stepwise approach begins with an accepted measure of efficiency. In this case, the method currently used by the bank to calculate branch efficiency is the cost/income ratio for each branch. The lower the value of this ratio, the more efficient the branch is considered to be.

However, the aim of DEA is to take account of all factors influencing performance, not just total income and total cost.

The second stage in Norman and Stoker's approach is to identify additional factors which influence a branch's performance. They seek to identify such factors by looking at the correlation between the income/cost ratio and other factors in the dataset. A high (positive or negative) correlation indicates that the factor in question is related to performance. If it is felt that there is a causal relationship between that factor and performance, then it is a candidate for inclusion in the DEA model; the factor having highest correlation is included in the model at the next step.

The next stage is to run the DEA model using total income (as an output), total cost (as an input) and the new factor (as an input or output, as appropriate). This is an iterative procedure which at each step measures efficiency in terms of the important factors identified up to that step. This process is repeated until no further important factors emerge. As a result of this process an efficiency measure which accounts for all the identifiable factors which influence performance will have been constructed.

The 1989/90 dataset contained various factors relating to the operation of the branches. From these factors, those which were identified by the stepwise approach as being the most influential in determining the performance of a branch were included in the model as inputs and outputs. The inputs which were found to influence performance were the number of business current accounts, the number of corporate current accounts and total expenditure broken down into its two principal components of salary and other expenditure. The outputs used were fee income, the margin on advances and the margin on deposits.

4.3 DEA results and analysis

The efficiency results given by the DEA model, for the 58 branches, are shown in table 1.

Table 1: Distribution of efficiency ratings

Efficiency rating	Number of branches	Category
100%	15	Efficient
90 – 99%	8	Marginally inefficient
75 – 89%	29	Distinctly inefficient
< 75%	6	

Fifteen branches were found to be efficient, with another eight being marginally inefficient. The remaining branches were distinctly inefficient and are unlikely to make themselves efficient in the short term. The efficiency ratings do not imply a ranking of the inefficient branches against some absolute scale, but rather indicate the degree of a branch's inefficiency when compared with those branches in its reference set. The reference set is the set of efficient branches to which the inefficient branch has been most directly compared in determining its efficiency rating. Each inefficient branch will have its own reference set of efficient branches, which will have a similar input/output mix to itself. The reference branches should therefore provide examples of good operating practice which the inefficient branch can learn from.

Branch 26 has the lowest efficiency rating in the dataset (61.6 per cent) when compared with its reference set of efficient branches 11, 25, 45, 48 and 58. This suggests that Branch 26 is only about 60 per cent as efficient as these branches. It should therefore be able to reduce the inputs it uses by about 40 per cent and still produce the same level of outputs. This information may act as a prompt to the user to identify factors which influence Branch 26's performance which have not been taken into account in the analysis. If there is a common factor affecting a number of branches, it may be worth incorporating it in further analysis. If no such factors come to light and the assessment of the branch as inefficient is felt to be justified, then the information provided by DEA can be used as a basis for setting targets for the branch. As a first step in setting targets for the inefficient branch, it should be compared with each of the branches in its reference set.

Figure 1 shows a comparison between Branch 26 and Branch 45, one of the branches in Branch 26's reference set.

Figure 1: Comparison between Branch 26 and Branch 45

The input and output values for Branch 26 have been scaled to equal 100. Branch 45's values are then expressed as a percentage of Branch 26's values, thus making for an easy comparison between the branches. Branch 45 has similar or slightly higher inputs than Branch 26. However, the output achieved is substantially greater. The 'margin on advances' of Branch 45 is over five times that of Branch 26, and fee income is over twice as high. In this case, the performance of Branch 45 would serve directly as a useful target for Branch 26, as it operates at approximately the same level of inputs.

Table 2 shows the targets and potential improvement that the DEA analysis suggests are possible for Branch 26.

Branch 26 should be able to reduce its expenditure on both salaries and other expenditure by about 38 per cent, and with a reduction in the number of business current accounts by 38 per cent and corporate current accounts by 52 per cent, still achieve the same level of output.

The output of the DEA analysis provides this information for all the relatively inefficient branches in the dataset.

Efficient branches can be subdivided into the robustly efficient and the marginally efficient, according to the number of reference sets they feature in. Branch 2 was found to be efficient and to act as a reference branch for 37 branches, which is over half the branches in the dataset. This branch can be held up as an exemplar of good performance. In contrast, Branch 48, which is also efficient, acts as a reference branch for only two branches. This suggests that Branch 48 may have an unusual mix of inputs/outputs which may prompt management to investigate why this is the case. It should be borne in mind that DMUs which are found to be efficient are relatively efficient in comparison with other units in the dataset. There may well be scope for efficiency gains in the efficient units, and this is more likely in units which do not have well-rounded performance.

Table 2: Targets for Branch 26

	Branch 26	Actual	Target	Potential improvement
Inputs	Business current accounts	717	441.0	38.4%
	Corporate current accounts	36	7.0	52.5%
	Other expenditure (£000)	449	276.6	38.4%
	Salary expenditure (£000)	308	190.0	38.4%
Outputs	Margin on advances (£000)	175	175.0	0%
	Margin on deposits (£000)	557	557.0	0%
	Fee income (£000)	185	185.0	0%

4.4 *DEA score and the cost/income ratio*

A principal argument for the use of DEA to measure the efficiency of bank branches is that it can take into account more factors than the simple cost/income ratio. It is, therefore, useful to examine the implications of this. Figure 2 is a plot of the DEA score against cost/income ratio for each branch.

The correlation between the two measurements is –0.71. In general, branches which score highly on DEA have a low cost/income ratio and vice-versa, as one would expect. However, there are exceptions, and there is also a wide variation between the cost/income ratios obtained for branches with a similar score. The plot is divided into four sections: the vertical line separates the efficient and marginally inefficient branches from the distinctly inefficient. The horizontal line is drawn at the average cost/income ratio. The branches lying in the bottom-right quadrant may be considered to be of little concern to management as they are performing well according to either method of measuring efficiency. Those in the top-left quadrant are relatively inefficient according to both methods. However, DEA goes a step beyond the simple ratio analysis in providing target information for each of these units. The branches in the other two quadrants are, perhaps, more of a surprise. Why would a branch with lower than average cost/income ratio be considered inefficient by the DEA analysis, and why would a branch with a higher than average cost/income ratio be considered efficient? The answer to the second question is easier than the first. DEA, in taking account of multiple inputs and outputs, allows greater opportunity for a branch to appear efficient. However, we do not have the answer to the first question. A variety of multivariate statistical analyses were carried out on the raw data, but no common link between these branches was discovered. It is unfortunate that we were not able to identify which branches they were in order to determine if there was an environmental factor which linked them.

Branch 59, indicated on the plot, stands out by virtue of having a high cost/income ratio of 0.86, the highest in the dataset, which implies inefficiency but also a relatively high DEA score of 86.2. This branch has the lowest salary costs, as a proportion of total expenditure, of any branch in the dataset, which accounts for its high DEA score. A closer look at the results for branch 59 indicate a problem with 'other expenditure'; the target set by DEA suggests that for branch 59 to be efficient it would need to reduce this expenditure by almost 60.

Drake and Howcroft (1994) in their DEA study of bank branches also considered the issue of whether the use of DEA in combination with the conventional financial ratios used by banks might provide additional insights. They suggest that the cost/income ratio shows management which branches have excessive costs in relation to the income that they generate, but that the particular sources of inefficiency are not revealed; DEA by contrast identifies which inputs are being used inefficiently and indicates in percentage terms how much each input could be reduced while still maintaining the same level of outputs.

Figure 2: Plot of cost/income ratio and DEA score

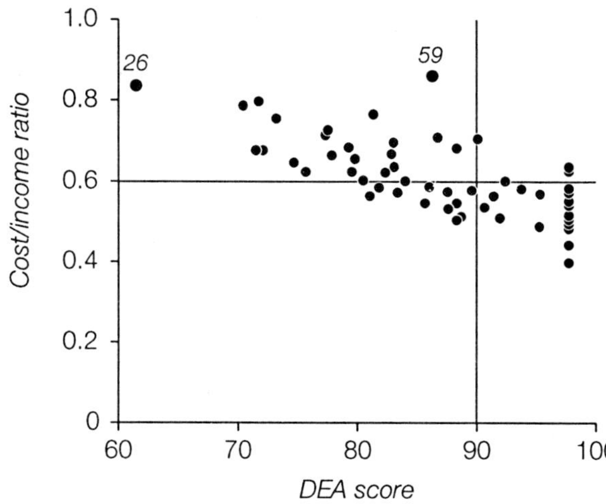

If DEA were to be used as a monitoring tool, then a number of useful comparisons could be made across years (or any other reporting period). It would be of interest to know if individual branches had become more, or less, efficient in comparison with their peers, and if there had been an overall improvement in efficiency from one period to the next.

5 View of bank staff on the use of DEA

The study was carried out principally in conjunction with a central management services department. The process and results have been discussed widely with management accounting and branch banking management staff. The objective of identifying efficient and inefficient branches in the bank is the focus of considerable effort, and as a result of this study DEA is seen as a potentially useful additional measure of branch performance. A number of issues emerged as a result of these discussions. The first concerned the availability of data and the need for it to be consistent and reliable. Although an extensive branch database had been recently developed, it did not contain some information thought to be relevant in assessing efficiency, in particular data on the number of transactions processed by a branch. It was felt that this information, reflecting volume of activity, would be a key output measure in assessing operational efficiency of branches.

The 'input minimisation' approach was adopted in this study: that is, for each inefficient branch we sought to identify the level of costs at which the existing level of revenue should be attainable. DEA, however, can also be used to assess the revenue potential of the branches. That is, given the costs that the branch incurs, what level of revenue should it have achieved? However, if the DEA models are to be used for this purpose, then factors which take account of the market potential would need to be incorporated into the models. These factors could include a measure of the competition that the bank branch faces from other banks in its location, and a measure of the branch's catchment population. Unfortunately, this data was not readily available and could not be obtained during the timescale of the study.

Another issue which arose was how to incorporate a measurement of risk in the analysis. Many of the potential measures of output generated by branches are related to the volume of activity (e.g. number of accounts, advances, margin on advances, etc.) but take no account of inherent risk. Institutionalising such an approach to efficiency measurement runs the risk of encouraging a branch manager to generate advances without due consideration of the risk involved. The need to measure risk, and the difficulty of doing so, is an issue relevant to any approach to performance measurement, not only DEA. An approach such as DEA, which explicitly incorporates multiple factors, facilitates the introduction of such a measure if one exists.

One of the bank's management accountants expressed the view that DEA is not a simple concept to explain. He considered that the principal of using cost/income to measure branch performance was widely accepted within the bank and that the introduction of an additional measure like DEA would require extensive training and familiarisation both on its calculation and interpretation. This is a reaction which has been encountered by one of the authors of this report in previous attempts to use DEA (*Belton*, 1992), and by other users. *Hellier* (1991) described similar reactions from management when DEA was used to assess the efficiency of Post Office Counters.

6 *Visual interactive DEA*

As a general means of overcoming this problem of perceived complexity, *Belton and Vickers* (1993) proposed a revised formulation of DEA, implemented as a visual interactive decision support system. DEA is presented in a way which is easy to understand, and the visual interactive implementation allows users to 'play', building their confidence in the approach.

A prototype system called Visual Interactive DEA (VIDEA) has been implemented, and the reaction of managers who have been shown the system is that it does help clarify the process.

The main display of the visual interactive system is the efficiency plot, which is shown in Figure 3. Each unit is represented in the plot by a square (use of colour facilitates identification of individual units in the actual system); a set of ten branches is used to illustrate the concept. The plot shows the aggregate output score (a weighted sum of a unit's scores on the individual output measures) on the vertical axis against the aggregate input score (a weighted sum of a unit's scores on the individual input measures) on the horizontal axis, for each unit.

Figure 3: Efficiency plot for Branch 13 with most balanced weights

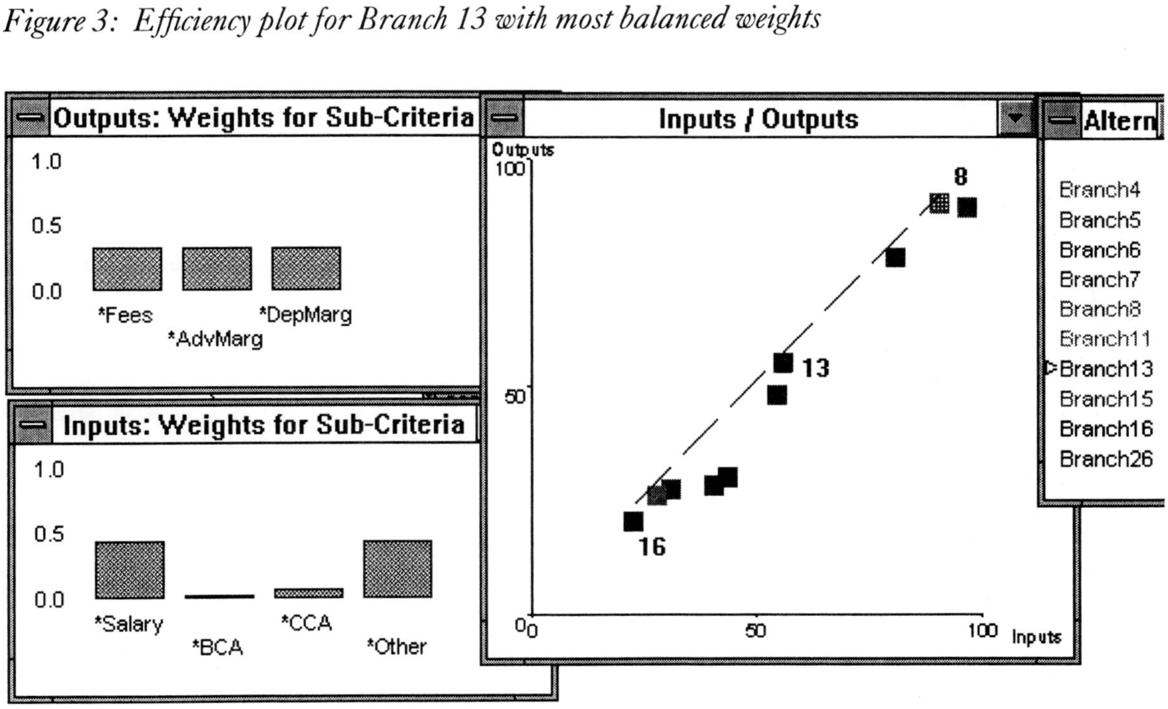

In determining whether or not a unit is efficient, the DEA analysis ascertains if there is a set of weights for inputs and outputs which put that particular unit on the efficiency frontier. This is the north-west frontier of the efficiency plot in Figure 3, shown by a dashed line. The weights used to calculate the aggregate scores currently displayed are shown in the bar charts alongside the efficiency plot.

The user selects which unit they want to investigate, and the results of the analysis are immediately displayed. Figure 3 actually shows the results of analysis for Branch 13; the weights shown are the most balanced values (i.e. as close to equality as possible) which make Branch 13 efficient. It can be seen that in order to achieve efficiency a low weight is given to both the number of business current accounts (BCA) and corporate current accounts (CCA). If users feel uncomfortable with this conclusion, they can interactively make changes to the weights and immediately see the implication for the unit's efficiency. Figure 4 shows that, as the weight on these two inputs is increased, Branch 13 moves away from the efficient frontier.

Figure 4: Efficiency plot for Branch 13 with changes to weights

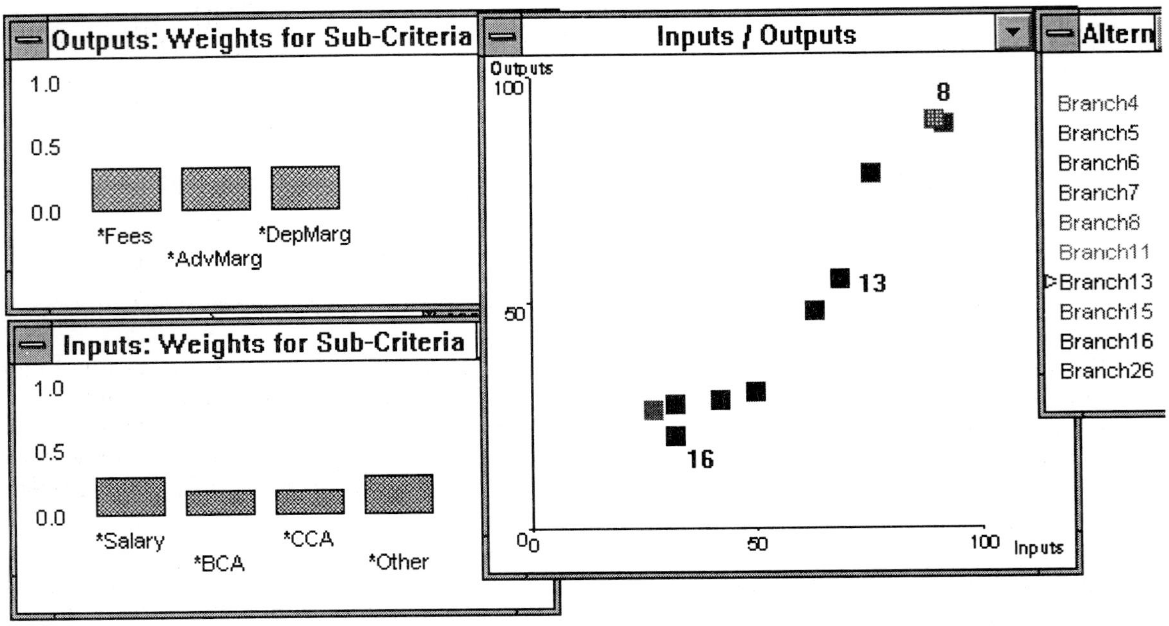

Figure 5: Efficiency plot for Branch 26

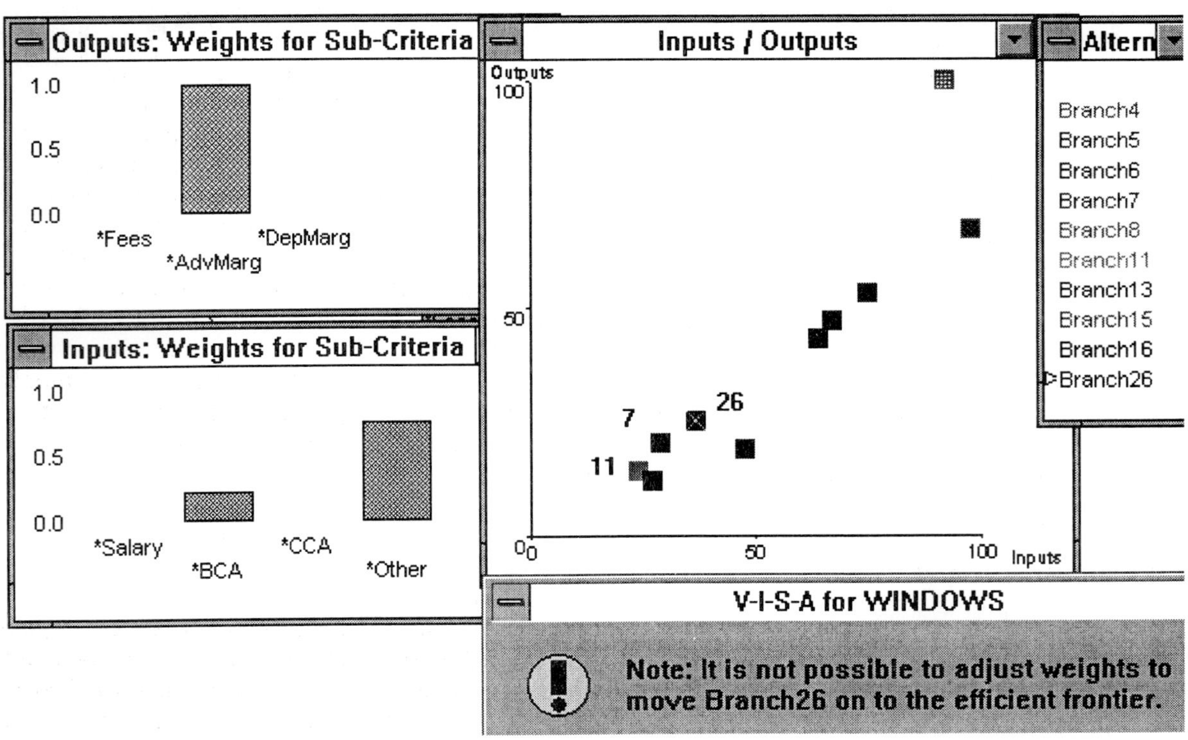

Figure 6: Comparison of Branches 7, 11 and 26

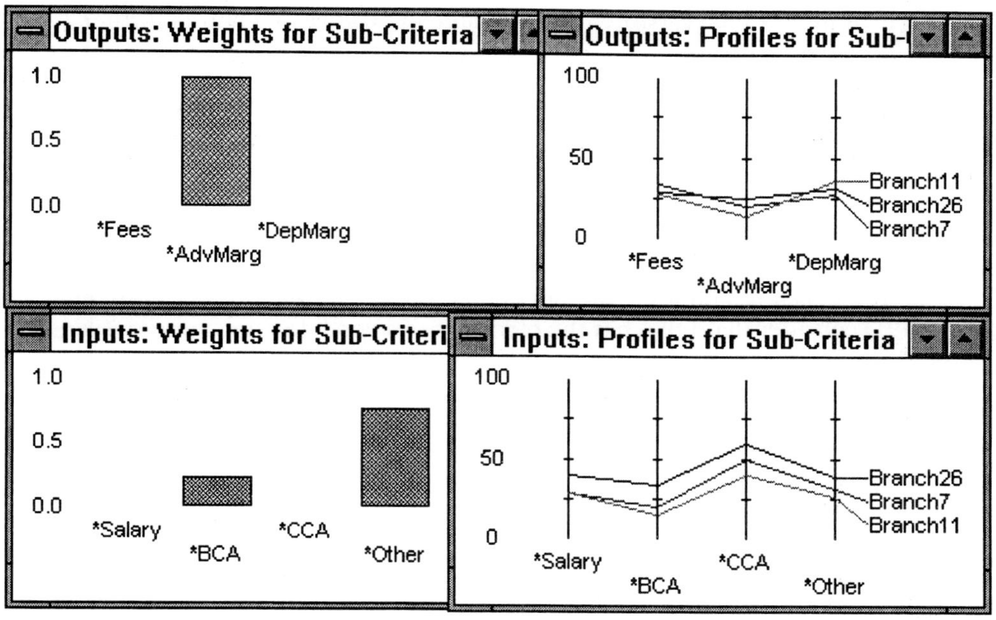

If a unit is inefficient, the analysis finds the set of weights which put it as close as possible to the efficient frontier. Figure 5 shows the output of analysis for Branch 26; although it is close, it is not actually on the efficient frontier. Figure 6 allows an easy comparison of Branch 26 with Branch 11 and Branch 7 which lie close to Branch 26, but on the efficient frontier. It shows that Branch 26 operates at a higher level of inputs than the other two branches, but achieves similar output levels.

Thus, the visual displays and interactivity service both as an effective vehicle for explaining DEA, making it appear less of a black box, and as a tool to support more in-depth analysis.

7 *Survey of CIMA members in financial institutions*

A survey of CIMA members who work in financial services institutions was carried out in order to determine the extent to which management accountants were already aware of the technique of DEA. A total of 244 questionnaires was sent out to those members working in financial institutions which were thought to be the most likely to have a branch network. The questionnaire sought to establish how much they already knew about the technique and, if they had used it, if they had found it useful. A response rate of 42 per cent was achieved. It was found that the number of members who had already heard of DEA prior to receiving the questionnaire was twelve, and of these members only three had actually tried using DEA. The three who had used it did find it useful, however, as they replied that they had used it to: 'target and monitor key tasks in the branch network where it was found to be extremely useful as a key performance indicator'; 'evaluate job efficiency, where it was found useful in providing a benchmark, but did not measure soft issues like environment, systems, personality etc.' and 'branch location analysis where the results obtained were found to be useful'. The survey found that the most commonly used methods of assessment were the financial ratios cost/income (72 per cent of respondents) and contribution (67 per cent). An interest was however expressed by 40 of the respondents in finding out more about the technique of DEA.

8 *Conclusion*

The aim of this study was to investigate the potential for DEA as a management accounting tool through its application to the evaluation of the efficiency of branches of a UK clearing bank. As the paper illustrates, a strength of DEA is that, in addition to identifying those units which are operating inefficiently in comparison with their peers, it suggests performance targets which are meaningful as they are derived from the actual performance of other units. The area of target setting is little explored in the DEA literature, but on the basis of this study the authors feel that it is an aspect of the technique which is particularly valuable in practice and merits further research.

By taking account of multiple factors in assessing performance, DEA helps identify areas of strength and weakness. Weaknesses can then be addressed to achieve an improved performance. Operating practices of units which exhibit strengths in particular areas can be examined to establish a guide to best practice.

DEA is a more complete and comprehensive method of assessing efficiency than a financial ratio such as cost/income. It yields more information, but demands more effort and commitment. *Desai and Walker* (1991) consider that DEA has the elements of a good decision-support system, but that currently its results are not readily grasped by managers. They suggest that it is the difficulty of visualising the results of the multidimensional analysis which leads to the lack of appreciation for its power. *El-Mahgary and Lahdelma* (1994) also argue that the lukewarm reception given to DEA by decision-makers is partly due to the fact that the results of a DEA analysis are difficult to convey. They suggest that its acceptance in the managerial community is hindered by a lack of suitable techniques for visualising the results. They propose various two-dimensional charts for illustrating the DEA efficiency results, and their hope is that the introduction of an increasing number of visualisation techniques will aid managerial understanding of the results.

The software tools which are currently available to support DEA on a large scale are such that it is unlikely they would be used directly by managers, or even used interactively in a management team with appropriate technical support. The visual interactive prototype system (VIDEA) described earlier has significant potential for advancement in this respect. In addition to VIDEA, efforts are being made to produce a Windows DEA software package which it is intended will be used to perform DEA analyses, visualise the results and support learning about the problem under consideration.

The management accountant presently seeking to adopt this approach for performance measurement must be analytically and technically well versed with the technique and supporting software. We hope that future developments will see the introduction of visual interactive software which will both increase usability and understanding of DEA at all levels. It is important, as with any analytical process, to involve interested parties at all stages of development, from the identification of relevant inputs, outputs and appropriate model type, through to the presentation and interpretation of results. Visual interactive software will facilitate this process.

Appendix

DEA evaluates the relative efficiency of decision-making units where the efficiency production function is not known or easily specified. In most cases there is no known relationship between the inputs used by an organisational unit and the outputs that it produces. The efficiency frontier is therefore not known. It can however be estimated by using the available data on the actual achieved performance, by the DMUs under consideration, in terms of the outputs that they produce for the level of inputs that they use.

DEA utilises a linear programming technique which maximises the efficiency of a unit subject to the efficiencies of all other units in the set having an upper bound of 1. The key feature is that the weights are chosen so as to maximise the efficiency of the individual unit. The efficiency of the unit will either equal 1 (100 per cent efficient) or will be less than 1, in which case the unit is inefficient. The relative efficiency score of a unit represents the maximum proportion of its inputs the unit should have been using, if efficient, in order to secure at least its current output levels.

The objective function of the DEA linear programming model is:

$$maxE_0 = \frac{\sum_{r=1}^{s} u_r y_{ro}}{\sum_{i=1}^{m} v_i x_{io}}$$

The constraints are:

$$\frac{\sum_{r=1}^{s} u_r y_{rj}}{\sum_{i=1}^{m} v_i x_{ij}} < 1$$

where $j = 1, \ldots, n$

and:

$$0 < u_r \quad r = 1, \ldots, s \qquad 0 < v_i \quad i = 1, \ldots, m.$$

Outputs: y_{rj} = observed amount of *r*th output for the *j*th unit.

Inputs: x_{ij} = observed amount of *i*th input for the *j*th unit.

References

Belton V. (1992), 'An IDEA – integrating data envelopment analysis with multiple criteria analysis', in *Proceedings of the Ninth International Conference on Multiple Criteria Decision Making: Theory and Applications in Business, Industry and Commerce* (eds. Gocoecha A., Duckstein L. and Zionts S.), pp. 71–79. Springer-Verlag, Berlin.

Belton V. and Vickers, S. (1993), 'Demystifying DEA: A visual interactive approach based on multiple criteria analysis', *Journal of the Operational Research Society*, Vol. 44, No. 9, pp. 883–896.

Banker R. D., Charnes A. and Cooper W. (1984), 'Some models for estimating technical and scale inefficiencies in date envelopment analysis', *Management Science*, 30/9, pp. 1078–1092.

Charnes A., Cooper W. and Rhodes E. (1978), 'Measuring the efficiency of decision making units', *European Journal of Operational Research*, 6, pp. 429–444.

Colwell R.J. and Davis E.P. (1992), 'Output and productivity in banking', *Scandinavian Journal of Economics*, 94, Supplement, pp. 111–129.

Deasi A. and Walters L.C. (1991) 'Graphical presentations of data envelopment analyses: management implications from parallel axes representations', *Decision Sciences*, Vol. 22, pp. 335–353.

Drake L. and Howcroft B. (1994), 'Relative efficiency in the branch network of a UK bank: an empirical study', *OMEGA International Journal of Management Science*, Vol. 22, No. 1, pp. 83–90.

El-Mahgary S. and Lahdelma R. (1994), *DEA: Visualising the results*, Working paper, Systems Analysis Laboratory, Helsinki University of Technology, Finland.

Farrell M.J. (1957), 'The measurement of productive efficiency', *Journal of the Royal Statistical Society*, Series A, 120, pp. 253–281.

Ganley G.A. and Cubbin J.S. (1992), *Public Sector Efficiency Measurement: Applications of Data Envelopment*, North-Holland.

Hellier M. (1991), *Data envelopment analysis in Post Office Counters*, Paper presented to APMOD 1991, Brunel University.

Miliotis P.A. (1992), 'Data envelopment analysis applied to electricity distribution districts', *Journal of the Operational Research Society*, Vol. 43, No. 5, pp. 549–555.

Norman M. and Stoker B. (1991), *Data Envelopment Analysis: The Assessment of Performance*, Wiley.

Oral M., Kettani O. and Yolalan R. (1992), 'An empirical study on analysing the productivity of bank branches', *IIE Transactions*, Vol. 24, No. 5, pp. 166–176.

Parkan C. (1987), 'Measuring the efficiency of service operations: An application to bank branches', *Engineering Costs and Production Economics*, 12, pp. 237–242.

Pastor J.T. (1993), *Efficiency of bank branches through DEA: The attracting of liabilities*, Working paper, Department of Maths, University of Alicante, Alicante, Spain.

Seiford L.M. (1990), *A bibliography of data envelopment analysis (1978-90)*, Technical report, Version 5.0, Department of Industrial Engineering, University of Massachusetts, Amherst, MA, USA.

Sherman H.D. (1984), 'Data envelopment analysis as a new managerial audit methodology: test and evaluation', *Auditing: A Journal of Practice and Theory*, Fall, pp. 35–53.

Sherman H.D. and Gold F. (1985), 'Bank branch operating efficiency: evaluation with data envelopment analysis', *Journal of Banking and Finance*, 9, pp. 297–315.

Thanassoulis E., Dyson R.G. and Foster M.J. (1987), 'Relative efficiency assessments using data envelopment analysis: An application to data on rates departments', *Journal of the Operational Research Society*, Vol. 38, No. 5, pp. 397–411.

Tomkins C. and Green R. (1988), 'An experiment in the use of data envelopment for evaluating the efficiency of UK university departments of accounting', *Financial Accountability and Management*, 4(2), pp. 147–164.

Vassiloglou M. and Giokas D. (1990), 'A study of the relative efficiency of bank branches: an application of data envelopment analysis', *Journal of the Operational Research Society*, Vol. 41, No. 7, pp. 591–597.

Criteria for Measuring Marketing Performance

Richard Wilson
(University of Technology, Loughborough)

Criteria for Measuring Marketing Performance

Introduction

In choosing among alternative courses of action or strategies it is desirable to choose the best, but how is the 'best' to be recognised? That which is best from the viewpoint of one stakeholder may not be best from another stakeholder's viewpoint. Similarly, what is best in the short term may not be best in the long term. Specifying the criteria by which choices are to be made among competing alternatives is a crucial step in working towards improved marketing performance.

It has traditionally been the case that financial criteria have dominated choice processes irrespective of the initial emphasis that may have been given to non-financial criteria. Recent changes in strategic thinking (as reported, for example, by *Munro and Cooper* (1989)) have suggested that the dominance of financial measures may no longer be appropriate. For instance, the emphasis placed by McDonald's on quality, service, cleanliness and value shows that a financial criterion is insufficient, although there will invariably be one or more financial measures within any enterprise's set of *critical success factors*.

A selection of the most important financial and non-financial criteria is given in Figure 1; many of them will be discussed in this paper.

Figure 1: Financial and non-financial criteria

Financial	*Non-financial*
Liquidity	Sales volume
Cash generation	Market share
Value added	Growth rate
Earnings per share	Competitive position
Shareholders' value	Consumer franchise
Share price	Risk exposure
Profit	Reliance on new products
Profitability	Customer satisfaction
Cost leadership	Sustainable competitive advantage

Within the marketing literature there is surprisingly little coverage of effectiveness (i.e. doing the right things) as opposed to efficiency (i.e. doing things right). However, it is implicit in the extensive coverage of efficiency that the results of marketing activities are effective: it is not suggested that effectiveness should be traded off for greater efficiency. Nevertheless, the preoccupation that has existed with inputs rather than outputs tends to mean that outputs such as increased sales revenue, greater market share, or higher profits are taken as being self-evident measures of effectiveness.

The various inputs and outputs cited in the literature on marketing efficiency include those shown in Figure 2:

Figure 2: Marketing efficiency criteria

Inputs		*Outputs*
Marketing expense		Profit
Investment		Sales value
Number and quality of	*Marketing*	Sales volume
employees	*activities*	Market share
Quality of decisions		Cash flow
Technology		Value added
Administrative support		Consumer franchise

If we consider market share to be an appropriate output measure, we can relate this to the BCG growth–share matrix and the PIMS model.

The growth–share matrix was developed for use in portfolio planning (i.e. to generate a balanced portfolio of business activities with reference to cash generation and cash use). Relative market share serves as a proxy for cash generation, with market growth acting as a proxy for cash use.

Market share as an output measure also features prominently in the PIMS model – see *Abell and Hammond* (1979), *Buzzell and Gale* (1987), *Day* (1990). ROI is the dependent variable in the PIMS model, with market share playing a key role in the following sequence:

(i) superior relative quality is established by a business for its products;

(ii) this superiority facilitates the building of market share;

(iii) greater share brings with it cost advantages due to higher volume and experience curve effects;

(iv) superior quality allows premium prices to be charged which, in association with lower costs, ensures higher profits.

Whatever measures of input and output are used in an attempt to assess efficiency – and Figure 2 only offers a limited number of each – the overriding emphasis is typically upon readily quantifiable factors. This gives a means of both asking and answering the question as to whether the enterprise is getting as much output per unit of input as it should, or whether the efficiency of marketing activities might be improved. As we have seen, however, this concern with 'doing things right' begs the question of whether the right things are being done, which requires a fuller consideration of marketing effectiveness. This is provided by such approaches as marketing audit and Bonoma's approach to assessing marketing programmes.

We shall proceed through this paper by examining a range of individual criteria and then look at more broadly based multiple-criteria approaches to evaluating alternatives. Among the individual criteria will be some of a financial nature (specifically relating to liquidity, cost leadership, profit/profitability, and shareholder value) and among the non-financial categories we shall review growth, sustainable competitive advantage, competitive position and consumer franchise.

Financial criteria

As a consequence of their widespread use, we shall consider a number of alternative financial criteria for assessing marketing performance. While financial criteria often have a conspicuous significance, they invariably reflect the partiality of financial measures in two respects:

- they are typically defined by someone looking through a 'financial filter' – accountants have neither a neutral nor a marketing perspective;

- they fail to embrace those aspects of marketing performance which cannot be represented in financial terms (i.e. accounting systems measure those things which can be measured by accounting systems).

Cash generation

Pool liquidity is a greater threat to the survival prospects of an enterprise than is poor profitability, hence it is vitally important in choosing a marketing strategy to consider carefully the cash flow implications of available alternatives. This can be vividly illustrated via the BCG growth–share matrix which classifies products into four categories: stars, question marks (or wildcats), dogs and cash cows. These are illustrated in Figure 3.

Figure 3: Product portfolio matrix

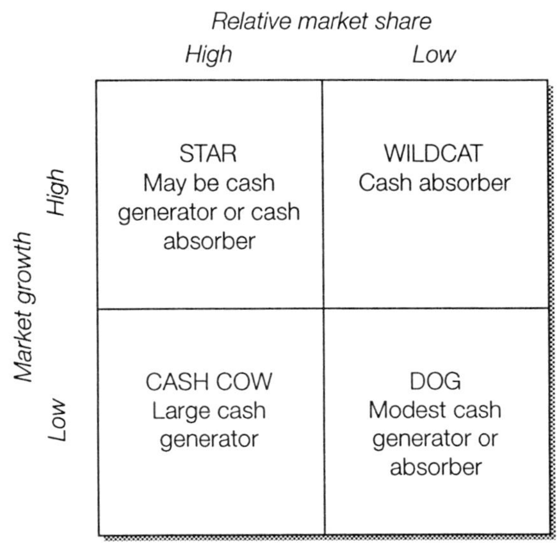

- *Stars* (high growth, high share) consume large amounts of cash in order to maintain their positions, but as leaders they also generate large amounts of cash. On balance there is unlikely to be any positive or negative cash flow until such time as the rate of market growth declines. At this stage, provided the share has been maintained, the product should become a cash cow.

- *Cash cows* (low growth, high share) should have high cash inflows with low costs, hence be net cash generators with limited reinvestment needs. The central importance of cash cows is evident when one considers that they cover payments of interest and dividends, and facilitate investment elsewhere in the business.

- *Dogs* (low growth, low share) have little in their favour – revenue generation is low and costs are high, hence cash generation is likely to be negative. It is easy to see that products in this category should be liquidated.

- *Wildcats* (high growth, low share) have even worse cash characteristics than dogs. The high growth requires high outlays, but the low share does not lead to low costs, so the wildcat is a net absorber of cash. If it can be developed into a star this may be a way forward, otherwise it should be divested. To become a star the share must be increased, which will require substantial investment, but lower costs should follow with a consequent net generation of cash over the longer term.

A typical business will have products spread across all four cells of this matrix. The strategy to be selected for each product must fit its position in the matrix seen against the overall picture. Thus cash cows will, in effect, subsidise products in other cells, wildcats will need to be supported if they are to achieve segmental dominance (failing which they should be liquidated), and so on. It is necessary to ensure that some products generate cash that can then be used to support growth if the overall portfolio is to be balanced.

By using the product portfolio as a frame of reference, this should ensure that all products, business units or profit centres are not treated alike, and that investment decisions are not seen as being independent of continuing business activities. Nevertheless, a strategic success sequence is likely to emerge through following these steps:

(i) The cash generated by cash cows (high market share, low market growth) should be invested in building the market share of wildcats. If this is done well, sustainable advantage will be provided by which wildcats will become stars and then cash cows, thereby being able to finance subsequent strategies.

(ii) To be avoided is the sequence by which wildcats are not supported so that they become dogs when the market matures: low relative share in a low-growth market is not the place to find oneself.

(iii) Also to be avoided is the sequence by which stars lose position and become wildcats as market growth slows, with the risk of their becoming dogs.

It should be mentioned that, in focusing on the balancing of operating cash flows, the BCG matrix ignores the existence of capital markets, which also have a role to play in balancing cash flows. Moreover, the BCG matrix fails to allow for differential risk.

Cost leadership

A particular strategy may be more desirable than others if it is likely to secure cost leadership (which is one of Porter's key generic strategies). This notion can be illustrated through the *experience curve.*

The essence of the experience curve is that the real costs of generating products and services decline by 20 per cent–30 per cent whenever cumulative experience doubles.

An important distinction needs to be drawn between the experience curve and the learning curve. The latter was initially observed during the 1920s and was a significant feature of the labour hours required for building aircraft during the Second World War – but it only relates to labour hours (hence labour cost). As a consequence, the reduction in costs due to the learning curve effect is much lower than that due to the broader-based experience curve. *All* costs and cost effects are reflected by the experience curve.

Several causes of cost reduction act together within the experience curve, such as:

- the learning experience;
- the effect of labour specialisation;
- scale effects due to increased volume.

The experience curve is derived not from accounting costs but by dividing the cumulative cash inputs by the cumulative output of end products, and the cost decline is shown by the rate of change in this ratio over time. From this rate of change managers can see how – and why – their competitive costs are shifting. If estimates can be made of competitors' experience curve effects, this should reveal which are the low-cost competitors and which are not, hence which are at risk and from whom.

The main strategic message from the experience curve is that, if costs per unit in real terms decrease predictably with cumulative output, then the market leader has the potential to achieve the lowest costs and the highest profits. This is illustrated in Figure 4.

Figure 4: Advantages of experience

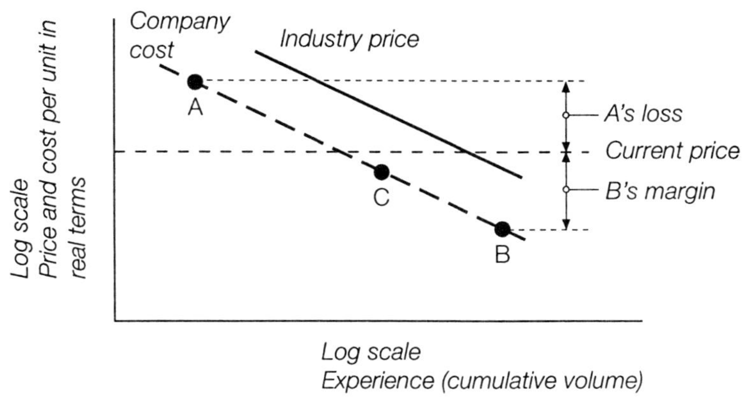

Firm A has less experience than Firm B, hence the latter has a significant cost advantage. In this rather extreme (but not implausible) example, A's unit cost is higher than the current market price, so it sustains a loss on each unit sold. By contrast, B's unit cost is well below the prevailing price, so it achieves a substantial margin on each unit sold. Firm C is operating profitably, but Firm B could take advantage of its leadership position in the following way: since the industry price falls with cumulative volume, Firm B can cut prices, as its costs also fall due to its greater experience. Firm A has virtually been driven out, and the same fate could befall Firm C.

Given the empirical existence of the experience curve, it is apparent that the use of cash will be less than directly proportional to a product's rate of growth. Similarly, the generation of cash will be a function of the product's market share, which links back to the BCG product portfolio matrix.

Profitability analysis

Profitability can be defined as the rate at which profit is generated: this may be expressed as profit (i.e. an output measure) per unit of input (e.g. investment, or some measure of effort such as sales calls). Apart from limiting our focus to one output measure (profit) to represent effectiveness, this approach also overlooks such issues as the quality of services rendered; its partiality thus needs to be kept in mind.

As a criterion for strategic decision-making, profitability has been criticised by *Robinson et al.* (1978), as being insufficient in:

- failing to provide a systematic explanation as to why one business sector has more favourable prospects than another and why one enterprise's position in a particular sector is strong or weak;
- not providing enough insight into the underlying dynamics and balance of an enterprise's individual business units and the balance among them.

Other writers, including *Chakravarthy* (1986) and *Day* (1990), have also criticised profitability as a performance criterion due to its remoteness from the actions that actually create value: it represents an outcome rather than a determinant of performance, and cannot be managed directly; hence employees are likely to attach limited importance to it on the grounds that their day-to-day actions would appear to have little impact on profitability.

Feder (1965) has defined good marketing performance as existing when investment in each market segment is made to the point where the expenditure of an additional $1 or £1 would produce greater immediate profits if spent elsewhere.

This approach reflects the *marginal responsiveness* that is characteristic of marketing experimentation (i.e. where can the greatest response in terms of improved profit be achieved for a marginal increase in effort?). To take an example, if investment of £1m in advertising within a given market produces sales of £20m and a gross margin of £10m, then the *average* response of profit to advertising is 10:1. If an increase in advertising expenditure of £100,000 produced additional sales of £3m and a gross margin of £1.5m, then the *marginal* response would be 15:1.

In assessing marketing performance using this approach, it would be logical to determine the average response for the existing allocation of marketing effort, segment by segment, which would highlight those areas in which the company has underspent or overspent relative to their profit potential. Improvements can be made by allocating additional effort in accordance with the anticipated marginal response: the greater the anticipated marginal response the more efficient will be the allocation of effort. In considering whether additional effort might be directed through direct selling, advertising, or improved terms for intermediaries within distribution channels, for example, the need exists to consider the timing factor, since different actions bring results over different time scales.

A less dynamic approach emphasising profit (rather than profitability) has been suggested by a number of writers. *Goodman* (1970) and *Pyne* (1984) both offer modified versions of financial operating statements as bases for assessing marketing performance. These are illustrated in Figures 5 and 6 (pages 72, 73).

In Figure 5, *Goodman* distinguishes carefully between direct and apportioned costs, which is a more relevant distinction than, say, that between fixed and variable costs if one is concerned to identify the performance of a marketing segment: relevance is given priority over the question of cost behaviour. In principle it makes sense to separate the profit attributable to manufacturing, distribution, and so forth, on a direct cost basis. The operational difficulty in doing this stems from the problems associated with identifying the direct costs of product 123 within a product range of 10,000 items.

Apart from the quantity of profits as a measure of performance, we might also consider the quality of profits. This depends upon the position of a particular product within its life cycle. It is evident that the profits from products in the growth phase of the cycle are likely to be more valuable than those in the decline phase, since the former have a more promising future.

Pyne's approach is similar in some respects to that of Goodman. For instance, both authors emphasise the need for conventional operating statements (i.e. those having a legalistic format) to be modified to reflect marketing's circumstances and, in so doing, to highlight direct costs.

In Figure 6 we can see that Pyne's approach differs in some significant ways from that of Goodman:

- revenue is analysed more fully;
- marketing costs are analysed more fully with headings that help in distinguishing operating from policy-related costs;
- the orientation is more radical than that of Goodman in giving a basis for assessing marketing performance in strategic terms.

The amount of profit an enterprise earns is a measure of its effectiveness if that enterprise has a profit objective. (In this sense we can define effectiveness in terms of achieving that which one sought to achieve.) Since profit = revenue (output) – cost (input), it can be seen to be a measure of efficiency also in that it relates outputs to inputs. Thus an organisation having revenues of £100m and costs of £60m is more efficient than one in the same industry having revenues of £100m and costs of £70m, since the former uses less input to produce a given output.

Despite its ability to act as a measure both of effectiveness and efficiency, profit is a less than perfect measure because:

- it is a monetary measure, and monetary measures do not measure all aspects of either input or output;
- the standards against which profits are judged may themselves be less than perfect;

- at best, profits are a measure of what has happened in the short run, whereas we must also be interested in the long-run consequences of management actions.

Nevertheless, profit measures can still play a distinctly valuable role in the control effort. For example:

- A profit measure can provide a simple criterion for evaluating alternatives. (Although it will be necessary to take into account many factors other than profit in making a choice among alternative courses of action, on the face of it option A is more attractive than option B if A will produce more profit than B.)

- A profit measure will permit a quantitative analysis of alternatives to be made in which benefits can be directly compared with costs. (Assuming a market exists for an enterprise's output, these benefits will be measured by the revenue flow from its sale.)

- A profit measure can provide a single, broad measure of performance in that it is arrived at after all financial costs and revenues have been taken into account, and it thus subsumes many other aspects of performance.

- Profit measures permit the comparison of performance to be made over time for one organisation, or comparisons at a point in time to be made for a group of organisational units (e.g. divisions or competing enterprises within an industry), even if they are performing dissimilar functions. This is not possible with other measures, although it may be necessary to standardise accounting practices in measuring profits for this purpose and to ensure that the valuations of assets are made on the same bases.

This all sounds very promising, but we need to bear in mind the limitations of the profit measure. Among these are:

- Organisations have multiple objectives and will often forego profit opportunities in order to avoid conflict over some other objective (or constraint), such as the desired image for the company or some ethical standard.

- Social costs and benefits are excluded from corporate profit figures. At best, profit is a measure of an enterprise's success as an economic entity, but this does not measure that enterprise's net contribution (or cost) to society, such as the training programmes it might offer, or the pollution it might cause.

- As already mentioned, profit measures typically focus on current rather than long-run performance: actions can be taken to improve the former at the expense of the latter (e.g. by cutting advertising, R & D, training and maintenance budgets).

- Profit is an inadequate basis for comparing organisations' relative performance or for monitoring one organisation's performance over time. The real test is actual versus target profit, but we are really unable to specify this latter figure in any sensible way because it should be based on *profit potential*, and a company's profit opportunities are not all identified. It follows that an apparently high profit figure, even when this corresponds with the target figure, may in reality be poor when related to missed opportunities.

- Accounting rules are also inadequate since they often do not permit the recording of economic reality. (Costs should reflect the use of resources, but accounting practice does not allow this to be measured when it values assets on the basis of historical cost rather than their opportunity cost, i.e. current value in an alternative use, which has an impact on the depreciation charge, etc.)

- Profit measures are not applicable in certain segments of a business, notably those that incur costs but do not generate revenue (unless a transfer pricing system is introduced to impute revenue flows). Examples of these types of segment are R & D, the legal department, the personnel department and the accounting department.

Figure 5: Marketing-oriented income statement

	£	£
Proceeds from sales		100.0
Variable cost of goods sold:		
Raw materials	10.0	
Packing	10.0	
Direct labour	5.0	
Variable gross profits (manufacturing contribution margin)		75.0
Other variable expenses:		
Freight	3.0	
Warehousing	2.0	
Spoilage	1.0	
Commissions	5.0	
Discounts	3.0	
Variable profit (distribution contribution margin)		61.0
Direct product costs:		
Advertising	9.0	
Promotion	3.0	
Direct product profits		49.0
Direct division costs:		
Sales management	12.0	
Product management	3.0	
Sales force	2.8	
Sales incentives	1.0	
Market research	0.2	
Division profit contribution (net contribution margin)		30.0
Allocated fixed expense:		
Factory indirect costs	21.0	
Supervision	4.0	
Other indirect costs	19.0	
Corporate administration	5.0	
Net division profit before taxes		(19.0)

(Source: Adapted from *Goodman* (1970), p.38).

Figure 6: Marketing-oriented profit statement

	£
Full revenue sales (at full sale price to end user)	*x*
Lost revenue	
Distributors' markups and margins	
Markdown, offers, deals and allowances	
Third-party costs of delivery to end user paid by the purchaser	
Sales proceeds	*x*
Sales taxes and customs duties	
Net sales proceeds	*x*
Direct marketing expense	
Direct selling: field sales expenses	
Sales promotion: merchandising and display	
samples, point of sales aids	
co-operative allowances to distributors	
Product packaging and branding expense	
Product services – installation, warranty and returns	
Warehousing – storage, receiving and marking, shipping	
Transportation outward – truck, rail, air; cost, insurance, freight and delivery	
Direct marketing contribution	*x*
Managed marketing expense	
Order processing	
Sales and distribution management	
Brand and product management	
Marketing direction and administration	
	x
Marketing policy costs	
Advertising and publicity	
Market research and customer relations	
Product planning, design and development	
Marketing team training and development	
	x
Committed marketing costs	
Inventory carrying – expense and financing	
Cost of credit – collection and financing	
Marketing equipment – maintenance, insurance, financing	
Net marketing contribution	*x*

Note. Where appropriate, lost revenue may be broken down by the marketing channels in use, e.g. wholesalers, stockists, retail chains, stores, direct vending outlets, etc.

(Source: *Pyne* (1984), p.90)

Creating shareholder value

Perhaps the majority of evaluative criteria advocated in the literature and used in practice focus on the maximisation of profit, profitability, or sales rather than on the return to shareholders (see, for example, *McGuire et al.* (1986), *Chakravarthy* (1986)). The key idea behind *creating shareholder value* (e.g. *Rappaport* (1986), *Wenner and LeBer* (1989), *Reimann* (1989)) is that investors only willingly invest in an enterprise when they think that the managers of that enterprise will be able to secure a better return on their funds than they could on their own without additional risk. In contrast to ROI and other short-term measures, the creation of shareholder value emphasises the market's assessment of the long-term health and wealth of the enterprise. Evidence exists to indicate that movements in an enterprise's share price are due (at least in part) to the impact of management's decisions on the long-term value of the enterprise. This is covered by the *efficient markets hypothesis,* which suggests that financial markets are adept at capturing information and reflecting the significance of that information in changes in share prices. It follows that decision-makers in enterprises having listed shares (which only applies to some 2,200 of more than one million companies incorporated in the UK) should pay due attention to the impacts of their decisions on share prices.

Day and Fahey (1988) have sought to demonstrate how a value-based approach can be applied to the evaluation of marketing strategies. The starting point is the recognition that value is only created when the financial benefits of a strategic activity exceed its costs. Since strategic activities are carried out over time – often involving several years – it is necessary to apply discounting methods to the relevant cash inflows and outflows. This is equivalent to the long-established practice of applying discounting techniques to new investments in plant and equipment: the extension of the practice to marketing strategies involves dealing with more intangible elements and embracing a series of issues rather than simply the investment in a single item of plant.

Non-financial criteria

We shall now turn from considering financial criteria to examine some criteria of a non-financial nature. There will often be financial consequences of non-financial criteria but, as in the case of growth, competitive position and so forth, non-financial approaches usually reflect dimensions which cannot be accommodated by financial measures.

Growth

The importance of growth as a criterion of choice stems from:

- Its relationship to gaining market share. Consider, for example, the sad case of the motorcycle industry in Britain. During the 1960s the level of output of British motorcycles was fairly constant (at 80,000 units p.a.) whereas the exports from Japan increased from 60,000 in 1960 to 2.5 million in 1973, with their production volumes tripling over this period. The British manufacturers failed to recognise the strategic importance of market share *on a worldwide basis* for long-term profitability related to the experience curve effect. While UK production during the 1960s ensured that manufacturing facilities were being adequately employed, the significant strategic issue was that Japanese manufacturers' costs were falling whereas those of British manufacturers were not, hence the collapse of the UK motorcycle industry in the early 1970s.

- The opportunities it provides for investment: as funds are generated they can be reinvested to produce a compound return.

Growth has a significant relevance to an enterprise's relative competitive position. This is most readily measured by relative market share, which is defined as the enterprise's market share divided by that of its largest competitor. Since the stronger the relative competitive position the higher the margins should be (due to the effect of the experience curve) this measure has a strategic importance.

The need for growth is shown in Figure 7, in which a gap can be discerned between the enterprise's present position and its preferred future position. By continuing with current activities on the same scale, the level of profits will decline (e.g. due to increasing competition, product obsolescence, etc.). By expanding in either existing markets (i.e. larger market share) or by entering new markets with existing products, or by improving existing products, it may be possible to maintain the level of profits into the future. (NB These alternatives employ known technology and, in two out of three cases, known markets.)

Figure 7: Gap analysis

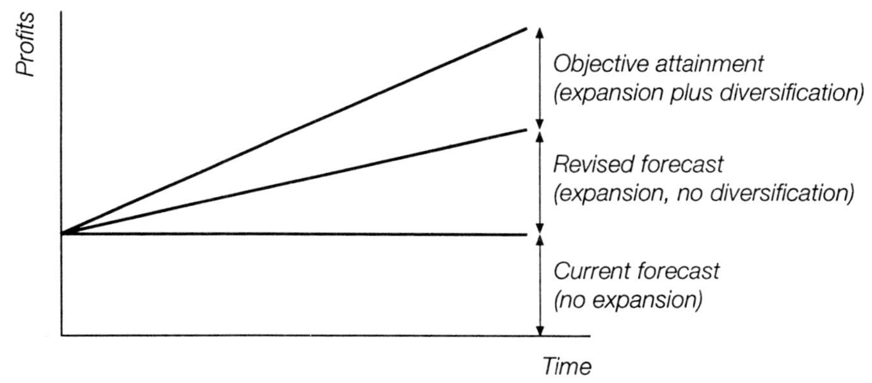

By expanding the scale of activity within existing markets, improving existing products *and* diversifying into new markets with new products, a much higher level of profit may result, thereby meeting the desired profit target. The choice of strategy, therefore, will be that by which the gaps in Figure 7 might be closed.

Growth will usually involve a move outside the enterprise's existing range of activities. Alternative paths for expansion are shown in Figure 8.

Figure 8: Growth strategies

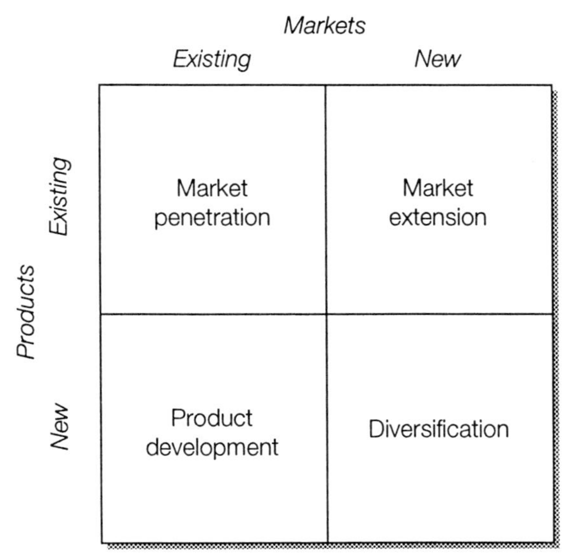

- *Market penetration* entails an increasing share of existing markets with existing products. This would involve more aggressive promotion and distribution.
- *Market extension* results from taking existing products into new markets.
- *Product development* requires that new products be created to replace existing products in present markets.
- *Diversification* involves the development (or acquisition) of new products for new markets.

The risk levels associated with these strategies tend to increase in the sequence in which they are listed above, so a change in product technology is likely to be riskier than a change in target markets, and a change in markets and products will be riskier than a change in only one of these (see Figure 9).

Figure 9: Orders of new product risk

Newness of market	Newness of product: Same product	Extended model	Modified or improved design	New product
Same market	1	2	4	8
Broader market coverage	2	4	8	16
New coverage in related areas	4	8	16	32
Totally new markets	8	16	32	64

Sustainable competitive advantage

Wensley (1981), *Day and Wensley* (1988) and *Cravens* (1988) argue that the most meaningful guidance for strategic decision-makers is to be found in returning to basics and focusing on the search for *sustainable competitive advantage*. This focus implies that strategic alternatives should be evaluated in terms of the organisation's strengths and weaknesses. Sustainable competitive advantage will be found when opportunities are taken to build on an enterprise's unique capabilities. These capabilities reflect the adequacy of the match between the current core activities of an enterprise and the strategic alternatives under consideration. Thus, for example, if we consider Ansoff's growth matrix (see Figure 8) an enterprise's greatest competitive advantage is likely to be found in product–market situations that are similar to those of its core activities (i.e. in cell 1).

A clear example is that of Gillette. Razors for men were followed by shaving cream for men and razors for women. Razors – whether for men or women – can be manufactured using the same facilities, and the marketing has similarities whether it is razors or shaving cream one is considering. A common brand name helps develop a consumer franchise. The distribution system in use for razors can also be used for shaving cream – the products are bought in the same outlets.

At first sight it may appear odd that Gillette ventured into disposable lighters, since they do not fit synergistically with the marketing of razors, etc. However, Gillette's special capabilities include:

- mass production of low-cost products;
- utilisation of precision plastic moulded parts;
- use of mass distribution;
- marketing of low cost, disposable consumer products under the Gillette brand name.

The manufacturing and marketing capabilities ensured that Gillette secured competitive advantage in disposable lighters even if the brand name itself was not particularly useful.

Competitive position

In considering financial criteria it is usually found that a rather introspective approach is adopted (i.e. this enterprise's profit, or this enterprise's cash flow). There is a need for adopting a more strategic perspective in dealing with an enterprise's competitive position.

The strategic dimension emerges when the performance of the business in question is compared with that of its competitors. Viewing the business within its competitive context is possible within the framework suggested by Figure 10.

Figure 10: Strategic comparisons

Economic performance of competitive units

	Market leader	*Dominant challenger*	*Own business unit*	*Closest competitors A*	*B*
Revenues					
Resource costs					

Source: Adapted from *Pyne* (1984), p.90

The details from Figure 6 would be entered in the rows of Figure 10 under the given headings.

A variation on this theme, focusing on the notion of competitive position, has been developed by *Simmonds* (1986). This is covered in some detail in the following discussion.

The key notion here is that of an enterprise's position *relative to* competitors' positions. In so far as strategy is concerned with competitive position it has been largely ignored by management accountants, but in a number of papers *Simmonds* (1981, 1982, 1985, 1986) has proposed how this failing might be overcome.

A basic plank in his argument is the preoccupation that accountants have with the recording, analysing and presentation of cost data relating to existing activities. This 'data orientation' begs some fundamental questions – such as why the data is being collected in the first place. An alternative and preferable approach is one of 'information orientation', which starts with the diagnosis of problems, leading to the structuring of decisions, and thence to the specification of information that will help in making appropriate decisions. The focus shifts from the analysis of costs *per se* to the value of information.

The manager wishing to make decisions that will safeguard his organisation's strategic position must know by whom, by how much, and why he is gaining or being beaten. In other words, strategic indicators of performance are required. Conventional measures, such as profit, will not suffice.

Let us take comparative costs as a starting point. It is intuitively the case that organisations having a cost advantage (i.e. lower unit cost for a product of comparable specification) are strong, and those having a cost disadvantage are weak. If we relate this to the idea of the experience curve (which was introduced on page 68 above) it will be appreciated that, if costs can be made to decline predictably with cumulative output, that enterprise which has produced most should have the lowest unit cost and, therefore, the highest profits.

Apart from cost, an enterprise may seek to gain strategic advantage via its pricing policy. In this setting the management accountant can attempt to assess each major competitor's cost structure and relate this to its prices – taking care to eliminate the effects of inflation from the figures being used. Applying cost-volume-profit analysis to one's competitors is likely to be more fruitful than simply applying it internally.

> *'Clearly, competitor reactions can substantially influence the outcome of a price move. Moreover, likely reactions may not be self-evident when each competitor faces a different cost-volume-profit situation. Competitors may not follow a price lead nor even march in perfect step as they each act to defend or build their own positions. For an adequate assessment of the likelihood of competitor price reactions, then, some calculation is needed of the impact of possible price moves on the performance of individual competitors. Such an assessment in turn requires an accounting approach that can depict both competitor cost-volume-profit situations and their financial resources.'* *(Simmonds [1982], p.207)*

After dealing with costs and prices, the next important (and related) variable to consider is volume – especially market share. By monitoring movements in market share, an enterprise can see whether it is gaining or losing position, and an examination of relative market shares will indicate the strength of different competitors.

Reporting market share details along with financial details can help in making managerial accounting reports more strategically relevant.

The significance of competitive position has been highlighted by *Simmonds* (1986) as being the basic determinant of future profits and of the business's value. Moreover, since competitive position can change over time, so can profits and value, but it should not be assumed that an improvement in competitive position will be associated with an improvement in short-run profits. In fact, the opposite is likely to be the case due to the need to incur costs in building up a competitive position, which has the effect of depressing current profits in favour of future profits. This raises the question as to whether competitive position can be measured in accounting terms – not just for a given business, but also for its main competitors; and not just at a point in time, but also over time. Simmonds has attempted to do this by applying strategic management accounting. He makes it clear, however, that it is not possible to express competitive position as a single figure. Instead, it is possible to offer an array of indicators relating to the competitive situation. From these indicators managers can gain insights into a business's competitive position, which will help them in judging whether or not things are moving in their favour.

After seeing the appeal of the approaches suggested by *Pyne* and *Simmonds*, one might wonder how the necessary competitive information might be gathered. *Brock* (1984), *Pyne* (1985), *Beerel* (1986), *Jones* (1988), *Robert* (1990), *Wilson* (1994) and others offer a variety of ways forward.

Consumer franchise

It has been argued (*Mehotra*, (1984)) that market share and profit measures are unsatisfactory for gauging efficiency, since they ignore the purpose of marketing, which he sees as being the identification of, and meeting, the needs and wants of end users. His proposed measure is *consumer franchise,* which he has developed from an approach within General Electric. The basis of this approach is to be found in a continuum, with consumers being arrayed along it in accordance with the probability of their buying a particular brand. An enterprise's core consumer franchise for its brand is represented by consumers having a consistently high probability of buying that brand. Those consumers with a low probability of buying that brand are likely to be either committed to another brand or uncommitted to any brand. It is apparent, therefore, that a brand's sales can be represented by the following equation:

$$\text{Sales} = (P_1 \times N_1) + (P_2 \times N_2)$$

where:
- P_1 is probability of buying if committed
- N_1 is number of committed buyers
- P_2 is probability of buying if uncommitted
- N_2 is number of uncommitted buyers.

The level of sales can be increased by increasing the probability of purchasing by a given consumer or by increasing the proportion of high-probability buyers – i.e. the consumer franchise. To achieve the former it is likely that sales promotion methods will be used, whereas advertising and product improvements are more likely for the latter. It can be argued that the use of sales promotions (as inputs) is likely to influence market share, but this may only be temporary. On the other hand, improvements in the consumer franchise are more likely to be lasting, hence a more desirable output. There is always a risk that some approaches to increasing market share (or sales or profit) may only achieve this in the short term and thereafter actually erode the consumer franchise – this would be reflected in a temporary improvement in efficiency but a reduction in effectiveness. In contrast, a brand's consumer franchise might be enhanced by a more substantive and co-ordinated improvement in the market offering.

Multiple criteria

Let us broaden our perspective and consider criteria that go beyond the single criterion approach we have been focusing on so far in this paper.

The use of a single criterion is inadequate because:

- organisations behave ineffectively from some points of view if a single criterion is used; *and*
- organisations fulfil multiple functions and have multiple goals, some of which may be in conflict. It would be inappropriate to assess strategies purely on the basis of any one criterion.

The difficulty, as will be apparent, lies in identifying those multiple criteria that are necessary and sufficient to ensure corporate well-being and survival. One way is via the application of Pareto's Law.

Pareto's Law (or the 80/20 rule) is widely thought to apply to a range of situations in which most of the behaviour or value of one factor is deemed to depend on only a little of another factor. For example, it is often asserted that 80 per cent of inventory movements within an organisation are attributable to 20 per cent of items stocked, 80 per cent of sales volume comes from 20 per cent of customers, or 80 per cent of profits are derived from 20 per cent of product lines. The main point here, of course, is that one can effectively control an inventory if one can focus attention on the critical 20 per cent of active items, or one can control the level of sales if the key customers are properly serviced. This can be greatly beneficial both in terms of cost savings (through eliminating unnecessary control effort on the 'insignificant' 80 per cent of items that only make up 20 per cent of stock issues) and in terms of improved organisational effectiveness (due to better control of the key elements).

The application of Pareto's Law is known by a number of different names. Perhaps the most frequently encountered are: key variables, critical success factors, and key result areas.

To illustrate the idea further we can consider a generalised example, and then a number of specific industry examples (see *Rockart* (1979)). Figure 11 identifies for each main sphere of activity the factors that are likely to be of some major significance to corporate performance. Each factor has financial implications, and if they can be controlled it is probable that the overall performance of the company can be controlled.

Figure 11: A general example of key variables

Sphere of activity	*Critical factors*
Environment	Economic – interest rates
	– inflation rates
	– concentration
	Political stability
Marketing	Sales volume
	Market share
	Gross margins
Production	Capacity utilisation
	Quality standards
Logistics	Capacity utilisation
	Level of service
Asset management	Return on investment
	Accounts receivable balance

Within specific industries there is likely to be considerable variation in key variables, as Figure 12 illustrates. *Johnson* (1967), for example, looks in more detail at this key question.

Figure 12: Specific industry examples of key variables

Food processing	New product development
	Good distribution
	Effective advertising
Motor vehicles	Styling
	Efficient dealer networks
	Tight control over manufacturing costs
Life assurance	Development of agency managerial personnel
	Effective control of clerical staff
	Innovation in creating new types of policies
Oil	Decentralisation
	Liquidity
	Government business relationships
	Societal image
	New ventures (to broaden its base)

The variables that are critical are those that are causally related to desired outcomes. In seeking to measure the values of variables, great care must be taken to avoid the trap of giving attention to variables that are amenable to measurement and overlooking more important variables that are not amenable to measurement (e.g. quantities are more readily measured than qualities, but it does not follow that the latter are less important than the former). Similarly, variables that reflect a short-run focus – such as reported profit or EPS – should not be allowed to dominate the measurement process when variables with a longer-run focus – such as competitive position – are being ignored in that process.

In a study of more than 250 US organisations, *Steiner* (1969) sought to determine the factors most likely to influence future success. He did this by asking the senior managers in the chosen companies to rank 85 factors. The top ten are shown in Figure 13.

Figure 13: Key factors influencing corporate success

1. Attract and maintain high-quality top management.
2. Develop future managers for domestic operations.
3. Motivate sufficient managerial drive for profits.
4. Assure better judgement, creativity, and imagination in decision-making at top management level.
5. Perceive new needs and opportunities for products.
6. Develop a better long-range planning programme.
7. Improve service to customers.
8. Provide a competitive return to shareholders.
9. Maximise the value of shareholders' investment.
10. Develop a better willingness to take risks with commensurate returns in what appear to be excellent new business opportunities in order to achieve growth objectives.

Source: *Steiner* (1969)

A variety of alternative approaches have been put forward for identifying key variables or critical success factors – see, for example, *Leidecker and Brun* (1984); *Jenster* (1987); *Freund* (1988); *Dace* (1990); *De Vasconcellos and Hambrick* (1989); *Hitt and Ireland* (1985). Such approaches usually rely on the views of managers and other experts within the particular industries. It is inherent in these approaches that their validity is questionable and that they do not constitute a clear basis for action. Is it helpful in the food processing industry, from the viewpoint of formulating action plans, to know that NPD, good distribution, and effective advertising are the prescribed critical success factors (as in Figure 12)? However plausible the CSFs might be, it is difficult to know how they will impact on an enterprise's competitive position.

An alternative approach that *Day and Wensley* (1988) argue gives more defensible insights is one that relates current sources of advantage to the achievement of advantageous competitive positions, hence superior performance. By relating causes (i.e. sources) to effects (i.e. performance) this approach emphasises linkages in a more explicit way (see Figure 14).

Figure 14: Comparing competitors

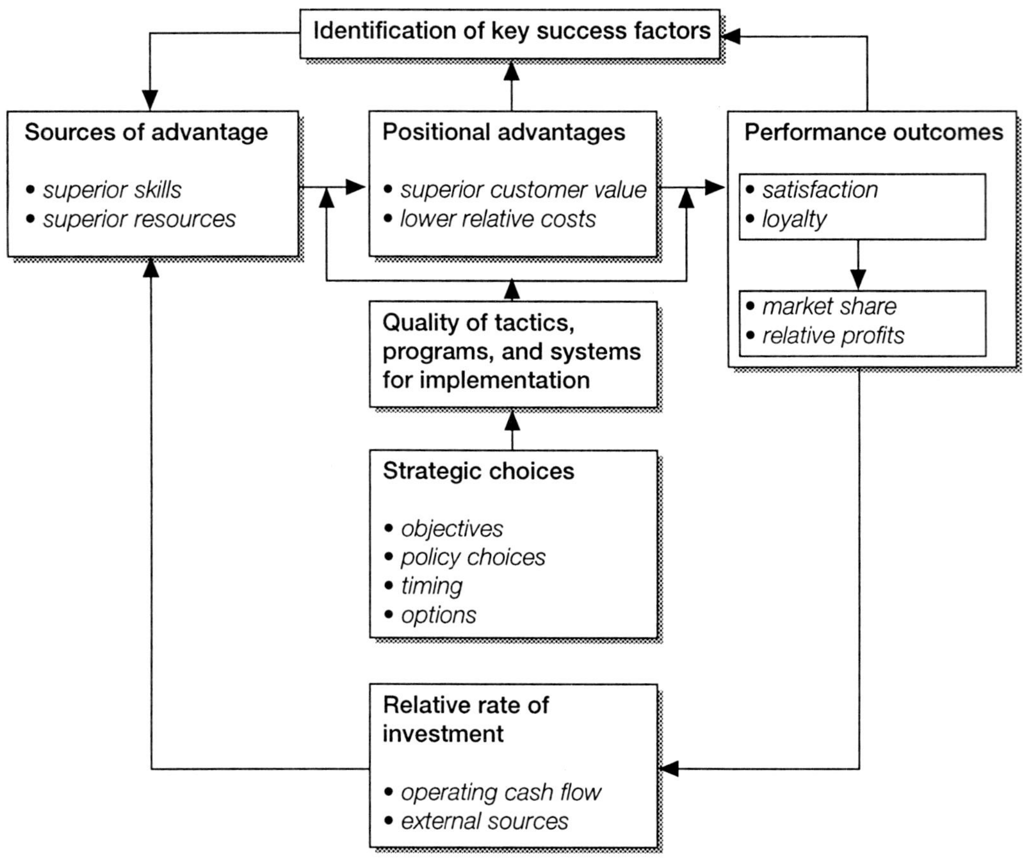

Source: *Day and Wensley* (1988), p.13

An example of operational linkages between CSFs and actions (in the form of specified strategies) is given by *Freund* (1988) for a life insurance company. These emerged from a process in which:

- top management identified what it considered were the company's CSFs;
- departmental managers then identified financial strategies that would allow the CSFs to be achieved.

While CSFs can serve as criteria for choosing among competing strategies, they are not equivalent to performance indicators. Figure 15 shows CSFs, a selection of strategies, and some performance indicators. The latter are designed to show when – and by how much – strategies are not being achieved once they have been implemented.

In a study of US companies, *D'Aveni and MacMillan* (1990) found that, under normal circumstances, managers in successful enterprises pay equal attention to their internal and external environments, but pay more attention to their output environment than to their input environment. When crises relating to demand decline arise, they focus their attention on the critical aspects of their external environment.

In contrast, the managers of enterprises that subsequently fail tend to ignore output factors during crises and pay more attention to their input and internal environment.

These results accord with the view that successful enterprises attend to critical success factors that relate to their output environments (e.g. customers' needs and demand growth).

Figure 15: Critical success factors in action

Critical success factor	*Strategies*	*Performance indicators*
Ability to achieve critical mass volumes through existing brokers and agents	• Develop closer ties with agents • Telemarket to brokers • Realign agents' compensation	• Policies in force • New business written • Percentage of business with existing brokers
Be able to introduce new products within six months of industry leaders	• Underwrite strategic joint ventures • Copy leaders' products • Improve underwriting skills	• Elapsed time to introduce • Percentage of products introduced within six months • Percentage of underwriters having additional certification
Be able to manage product and product-line profitability	• Segment investment portfolio • Improve cost accounting • Closely manage loss ratio	• Return on portfolio segments • Actual product cost/revenue against plan • Loss ratio relative to competitors

Adapted from *Freund* (1988), pp. 22–3

Relationships between CSFs (described as *corporate distinctive competencies*) and overall performance were examined by *Hitt and Ireland* (1985) in 185 US industrial enterprises. Their results suggested that distinctive competencies associated with performance vary according to the 'grand strategy' used on the one hand, and on the industry in which the enterprise is based on the other. A grand strategy refers to a predominant strategy covering the whole enterprise, and the view put forward by Hitt and Ireland for testing was that an enterprise should develop distinctive competencies in activities that are important from the point of view of implementing the grand strategy. They distinguish four industry types:

- consumer durables;
- consumer non-durables;
- capital goods;
- producer goods (e.g. raw materials).

The message that emerges from this work is that managers should be concerned to develop distinctive competencies that are appropriate for implementing their grand strategies within the context of their particular industries. It is important to match these matters in a balanced way.

It will be apparent that the choice of variables is neither neutral nor objective: in choosing what to measure, the manager is indicating his/her personal view regarding factors that are considered important in the control process. This can be illustrated via the well-documented (e.g. *Lewis* (1955); *Greenwood* (1979)) case of the American company, General Electric (GE).

GE set up a major measurement project which had three principal component parts dealing with:

(i) measures designed to assess the overall performance of a department or division as an economic entity;

(ii) measures designed to assess the performance of the functional activities within the organisation (such as engineering, production, marketing, finance, employee relations, and community relations);

(iii) measures designed to assess the performance of departmental or divisional managers.

The overall measurement project was based on the following principles:

- measures should be designed to provide factual inputs to support judgements in appraising the performance of departments or divisions;
- measures should be designed so as to provide performance indicators relating both to short-run and long-run goals;
- a minimum number of measures should be used at each level within an organisation.

In order to determine whether or not a variable qualified as a key success factor (which would require it to be measured), the following question was asked:

> *'Will continued failure in this area prevent the attainment of management's responsibility for advancing General Electric as a leader in a strong, competitive economy, even though results in all other key result areas are good?'*

A range of eight key success factors emerged from this project – see Figure 16.

Figure 16: General Electric's key result areas

1. Profitability
2. Market position
3. Productivity
4. Product leadership
5. Personnel development
6. Employee attitudes
7. Public responsibility
8. Balance between short-run and long-run goals.

While these eight factors might seem to be generally applicable, it is their precise definition within the context of a particular company's activities that determines how critical they are. This highlights a fundamental aspect of designing any control system: it must be highly 'situational' if it is to be effective. In other words, it must be tailored to the specific characteristics of the situation, which means *this* company's objectives, *this* company's operations, *this* company's managers, and *this* company's environment.

The General Electric approach seeks to balance two conflicting tendencies: on the one hand, the diffusion of effort over multiple goals and the failure to perform as well as might be expected in any one area; and on the other hand, the tendency to emphasise one particular goal with the result that other goals are not attained.

The most common tendency in commercial enterprises is to focus on the short-run maximisation of net profit (or sales) without considering the damage that this might do to the long-run position (e.g. by postponing repairs or maintenance work; by cutting back on advertising or on research, training or quality control expenditure; by deferring capital investment outlays; or through exhortations to employees to increase productivity). Short-term 'gains' achieved in this way tend to be illusory because the subsequent need to make up lost ground (e.g. via heavier advertising or training in later periods) more than outweighs the short-term gains.

To the extent that effectiveness is a multiple criterion, we must avoid the trap of focusing too sharply on one contributing factor. It would be a mistake to assume that effectiveness would be assured simply through selecting and training the right people. Given our definition of effectiveness, it may be assessed in terms of a system's capacity:

(i) to survive, adapt, maintain itself, and grow – regardless of the functions it fulfils; and

(ii) to achieve (i) through its bargaining position with its environment in relation to the acquisition of resources.

Against this background of criteria for effectiveness at an enterprise level, it can be argued that any attempt to deal with the effectiveness of individual elements of marketing – such as advertising or personal selling – is problematic for two major reasons:

(i) it is not possible to separate the impact of, say, advertising on the attainment of goals from the impacts of other elements of the marketing mix. The interdependence of the elements of the mix ensures that the selling task is influenced by advertising and by the nature of the product, the price and the channel decisions, all on a *mutatis mutandis* basis. It would not be sensible, therefore, to attempt to consider marketing effectiveness at any level below that of the marketing programme (i.e. the integrated set of marketing activities embracing the entire mix formulated to pursue a given strategy directed at a particular segment);

(ii) most criterion measures relating to individual elements of marketing are measures of efficiency rather than effectiveness, focusing on the maximisation of output for a given input, or the minimisation of input to achieve a given level of output. One exception to this is the use of sales quotas which represent output measures, and performance is assessed by reviewing how close each sales person came to achieving his/her quota. We can see that this is a measure of effectiveness, albeit on a small scale relative to the overall scheme of things.

With these caveats in mind, it is possible to identify criteria that are regularly applied in choosing among alternative plans for specific elements of the mix (see, for example, *McNamee* (1988), pp.131 and 143; *Guiltinan and Paul* (1988), pp. 396–8). Examples include the following:

Figure 17: Criteria for functional activities

Activity	*Criteria*
• New product programmes	Trial rate
	Repurchase rate
• Product programmes	Contribution margin
	Controllable margin as % of sales
• Sales programmes	Contribution by region, salesperson
	Controllable margin as % of sales
	Number of new accounts
	Travel costs
• Advertising programmes	Awareness levels
	Attribute ratings
	Cost levels
• Promotion programmes	Redemption rates
	Displacement rates
	Stock-up rates
• Pricing programmes	Price relative to industry average
	Price elasticity of demand
• Distribution programmes	Number of distributors carrying the product

Summary

In this paper we have looked at a range of possible criteria for assessing marketing strategies as a basis for making choices. Distinctions have been made among:

- short-term *v* long-term criteria;
- financial *v* non-financial criteria;
- single *v* multiple criteria;
- criteria focusing on overall strategies *v* criteria focusing on specific activities;
- criteria focusing on efficiency *v* criteria focusing on effectiveness.

Apart from the variety of input and output measures that have been discussed, there are additional approaches that deal with factors ranging from the degree of realism in the assumptions underlying the strategy to the capacity of the enterprise to successfully implement the chosen strategy. To take specific examples, *Tilles* (1963) and *Day* (1990) both outline sets of criteria that might be applied in assessing strategies. These include:

1. Is there an effective matching of the enterprise's competencies with the threats and opportunities from the environment? (If not, then there is unlikely to be a basis for achieving sustainable competitive advantage.)
2. Will the strategy place the enterprise in a position to counter known threats, exploit opportunities, enhance current advantages, or provide new sources of advantage?
3. Is the strategy robust enough to adapt to a broad range of anticipated environmental events, or is it only likely to work under very specific conditions?
4. Will it be difficult for competitors to deal with the expected advantages to be gained from the strategy?
5. Are the assumptions underlying the formulation of competing strategies realistic? (Such assumptions might relate to price levels, relative market share, market growth, cost levels, timing aspects, competitive reactions, and so on.)
6. What are the potential risks to which the strategy (hence the enterprise) may be vulnerable? (These may be internal – in the form of resource availability or implementation factors – as well as external.)
7. Is the strategy feasible from the viewpoint of the enterprise having the necessary skills and resources? (These would include access to technology, markets, and servicing facilities as well as adequate managerial capabilities.)
8. Is the strategy capable of being effectively communicated so that those who will be responsible for its implementation can understand what is required of them?
9. Will the strategy challenge and motivate key personnel? (This implies that strategies must be accepted by those who are charged with their implementation.)
10. Are the elements within the strategy internally consistent so that it hangs together in a coherent way?
11. Will the expected results from the strategy be acceptable relative to the anticipated risks? (This will require evidence of a clear competitive advantage from which enhanced value to shareholders and other stakeholders' gains will flow.)

12. Does the strategy have an appropriate time frame? (Strategies cannot be achieved overnight, so sufficient time must be allowed for their effective implementation.)

    What is needed is a balance among the variety of stakeholders' competing interests with their inherent conflicts and inevitable constraints. This need is vividly captured in Mintzberg's use of the verb 'crafting' in connection with strategy formulation. The same logic applies to assessing strategic performance.

    Our level of understanding of marketing processes is too limited for us to realistically seek to optimise outcomes, and the limitation of single criterion approaches to performance measurement in marketing are such as to favour a multiple-criteria approach – despite the need to proceed on the basis of heuristics rather than algorithms.

References

Abell, D.F. and Hammond, J.S. (1979), *Strategic Market Planning: Problems and Analytical Approaches*, Englewood Cliffs, NJ: Prentice-Hall.

Ansoff, H.I. (1968), *Corporate Strategy*, Harmondsworth: Penguin Books.

Beerel, A. (1986), 'Strategic Financial Control Can Provide Light and Guidance', *Accountancy*, Vol. 97, No. 1114, June, pp. 70–74.

Brock, J.J. (1984), 'Competitor Analysis: Some Practical Approaches', *Industrial Marketing Management*, Vol. 13, pp. 225–231.

Buzzell, R.D. and Gale, B.T. (1987), *The PIMS Principles: Linking Strategy to Performance*, New York: Free Press.

Chakravarthy, B.S. (1986), 'Measuring Strategic Performance', *Strategic Management Journal*, Vol. 7, pp. 437–458.

Cravens, D.W. (1988), 'Gaining Strategic Marketing Advantage', *Business Horizons*, Vol. 31, No. 5, pp. 44–54.

Dace, R.W. (1990), 'Exporting to Japan – Key Factors for Success', *Quarterly Review of Marketing*, Vol. 16, No. 1, October, pp. 1–7.

D'Aveni, R.A. and MacMillan, I.D. (1991), 'Crisis and the Content of Managerial Communications: A Study of the Focus of Attention of Top Managers in Surviving and Failing Firms', *Administrative Science Quarterly*, Vol. 35, No. 4, December, pp. 634–657.

Day, G.S. (1990), *Market-driven Strategy*, New York: Free Press.

Day, G.S. and Fahey, L. (1988), 'Valuing Market Strategies', *Journal of Marketing*, Vol. 52, No. 3, July, pp. 45–57.

Day, G.S. and Wensley, J.R.C. (1988), 'Assessing Advantage: a Framework for Diagnosing Competitive Superiority', *Journal of Marketing*, Vol. 52, No. 2, April, pp. 1–20.

De Vasconcellos, J.A.S. and Hambrick, D.C. (1989), 'Key Success Factors: Test of a General Theory in the Mature Industrial Product Sector', *Strategic Management Journal*, Vol. 10, No. 4, pp. 367–382.

Feder, R.A. (1965), 'How to Measure Marketing Performance', *Harvard Business Review*, Vol. 43, No. 3, May-June, pp. 132–142.

Freund, Y.P. (1988), 'Critical Success Factors', *Planning Review*, Vol. 16, No. 4, July-August, pp. 20–23.

Goodman, S.R. (1970), *Techniques of Profitability Analysis*, New York: Wiley.

Greenwood, R.G. (1974), *Managerial Decentralisation: A Study of the General Electric Philosophy*, Lexington, Mass.: D C Heath.

Guiltinan, J.P. and Paul, G.W. (1988), *Marketing Management: Strategies and Programs*, New York: McGraw-Hill (3rd edition).

Hitt, M.A. and Ireland, R.D. (1985), 'Corporate Distinctive Competence, Strategy, Industry and Performance', *Strategic Management Journal*, Vol. 6, pp. 273–293.

Jenster, P.V. (1987), 'Using Critical Success Factors in Planning', *Long Range Planning*, Vol. 20, No. 4, pp. 102–109.

Johnson, H.G. (1967), 'Key Item Control', *Management Services*, Vol. 4, No. 1, Jan-Feb, pp. 21–26.

Jones, L. (1988), 'Competitor Cost Analysis at Caterpillar', *Management Accounting* (IMA), Vol. 70, No. 4, October, pp. 32–38.

Leidecker, J.K. and Bruno, A.V. (1984), 'Identifying and Using Critical Success Factors', *Long Range Planning*, Vol. 17, February, pp. 23–32.

Lewis, R.W. (1955), 'Measuring, Reporting and Appraising Results of Operations with Reference to Goals, Plans and Budgets', *Planning, Managing and Measuring: a Case Study of Management, Planning and Control at General Electric Company*, New York: The Controllership Foundation.

McGuire, J., Schneeweis, T. and Hill, J. (1986), 'An Analysis of Alternative Measures of Strategic Performance', pp. 127–154 in Lamb, R. and Shrivastava, P. (eds.) (1986), *Advances in Strategic Management*, Greenwich, Conn.: JAI Press, Vol. 4.

McNamee, P. (1988), *Management Accounting: Strategic Planning and Marketing*, Oxford: Butterworth Heinemann.

Mehotra, S. (1984), 'How to Measure Marketing Productivity', *Journal of Advertising Research*, Vol. 24, No. 3, pp. 9–15.

Munro, R.J.B. and Cooper, P. (1989), *The Impact of Changes in Strategic Thinking on Management Control Systems: the Selection of Non-Financial Measures in a Functional Structure*. Paper given at the Annual Conference of the British Accounting Association, University of Bath, March.

Porter, M.E. (1980), *Competitive Strategy*, New York: Free Press.

Pyne, F.G. (1984), 'Better Operating Statements for the Marketing Director', *Accountancy*, Vol. 95, No. 1086, February, pp. 87–90.

Pyne, F.G. (1985), 'Accountancy that Helps to Meet and Beat Competition', *Accountancy*, Vol. 96, No. 1104, August, pp. 104–107.

Rappaport, A. (1986), *Creating Shareholder Value: the New Standard for Business Performance*, New York: Free Press.

Reimann, B.C. (1989), *Managing for Value*, Oxford: Basil Blackwell.

Robert, M.M. (1990), 'Managing Your Competitor's Strategy', *Journal of Business Strategy*, Vol. 11, No. 2, pp. 24–28.

Robinson, S.J.Q., Hichens, R.E. and Wade, D.P. (1978), 'The Directional Policy Matrix – Tool for Strategic Planning', *Long Range Planning*, Vol. 11, No. 3, June, pp. 8–15.

Rockart, J.F. (1979), 'Chief Executives Define Their Own Data Needs', *Harvard Business Review*, Vol. 57, No. 2, March\April, pp. 81–93.

Simmonds, K. (1981), 'Strategic Management Accounting', *Management Accounting* (CIMA), Vol. 59, No. 4, April, pp. 26–29.

Simmonds, K. (1982), 'Strategic Management Accounting for Pricing: a Case Example', *Accounting and Business Research*, Vol. 12, No. 47, Summer, pp. 206–214.

Simmonds, K. (1985), 'How to Compete', *Management Today*, August, pp. 39–43, 84.

Simmonds, K. (1986), 'The Accounting Assessment of Competitive Position', *European Journal of Marketing*, Vol. 20, No. 1, pp. 16–31.

Steiner, G. (1969), *Strategic Factors in Business Success*, New York: FERF.

Tilles, S. (1963), 'How to Evaluate Corporate Strategy', *Harvard Business Review*, Vol. 41, No. 4, July-August, pp. 111–121.

Wenner, D.L. and LeBer, R.W. (1989), 'Managing Shareholder Value – From Top to Bottom', *Harvard Business Review*, Vol. 67, No. 6, November-December, pp. 1–8.

Wensley, J.R.C. (1981), 'Strategic Marketing: Betas, Boxes or Basics', *Journal of Marketing*, Vol. 45, No. 3, Summer, pp. 173–183.

Wilson, R.M.S. (1973), *Management Controls and Marketing Planning*, London: Heinemann.

Wilson, R.M.S. (ed.) (1981), *Financial Dimensions of Marketing* (2 volumes), London: Macmillan.

Wilson, R.M.S. (1994), 'Competitor Analysis', *Management Accounting* (CIMA), Vol. 72, April, pp. 24–6.

Wilson, R.M.S. and Gilligan, C.T. (forthcoming), *Strategic Marketing Control*, Oxford: Butterworth-Heinemann.

Problems Arising from the Use of a Conventional AIS for Project Control

David Woodward
(Staffordshire University Business School)

Stephen Squires
(Independent Project Claims Specialist)

Problems Arising from the Use of a Conventional AIS for Project Control

1 *Introduction*

This paper presents findings from an examination of the accounting information system (AIS) operated by a company engaged in the construction industry, specifically in relation to a large project whose success is critical to the company's future. A case study[1] approach is utilised to illustrate both the use and abuse of the AIS by the company's managers.

The company's managing director (MD) is geographically remote from the project and is consequently reliant upon the information produced by the company's 'conventional' AIS as an adequate measure of results. However, the company's reward structure suggests the possibility of opportunistic behaviour on the part of the project manager (PM) in charge of the project, leading to the potential for bias and budgetary slack which the MD may be unable to detect, given his inability to directly monitor the effort expended by the project manager in his managing of the project. Given the scale of the project (it is the largest contract ever undertaken by the company), doubt also attaches to the quality of the predictive model of eventual outcome being used.

The paper is divided into three parts.

Section 2 uses a case study approach to examine in detail the dynamics of the company, and more particularly the project which is the focus of attention. This approach facilitates a 'teasing out' of some of the more obtuse and complex elements of the superior/subordinate relationship encountered in a project control situation. The derivation of the costing information used by the company is also demonstrated, with particular emphasis being placed on the scope which exists for abuse of that system.

Section 3 develops a theoretical perspective from which it is possible to examine the situation which arose within the company and permits some level of deduction as to why the situation was allowed to occur.

Sections 4 and 5 develop normative suggestions for the design of an improved AIS which, it is postulated, has potential applicability both within the object company and in others facing similar socio-economic conditions.

2 *Corporate dynamics and the project*

2.1 *The company*

The company (its identify is confidential) is engaged in two principal activities: the design, supply and installation of passive fire protection to buildings and structures, and the installation of dry-lining systems. At the time the project which is the focus of present attention was entered into, the company was 'close', with over 62 per cent of the issued shares being held equally by the two founder-directors.

Figure 1 provides financial highlights from the company's annual report for the year ended 28 February 1991 (at which time the project was ongoing), and gives the impression of a high-performing company.

Figure 1: Company profile, 1991

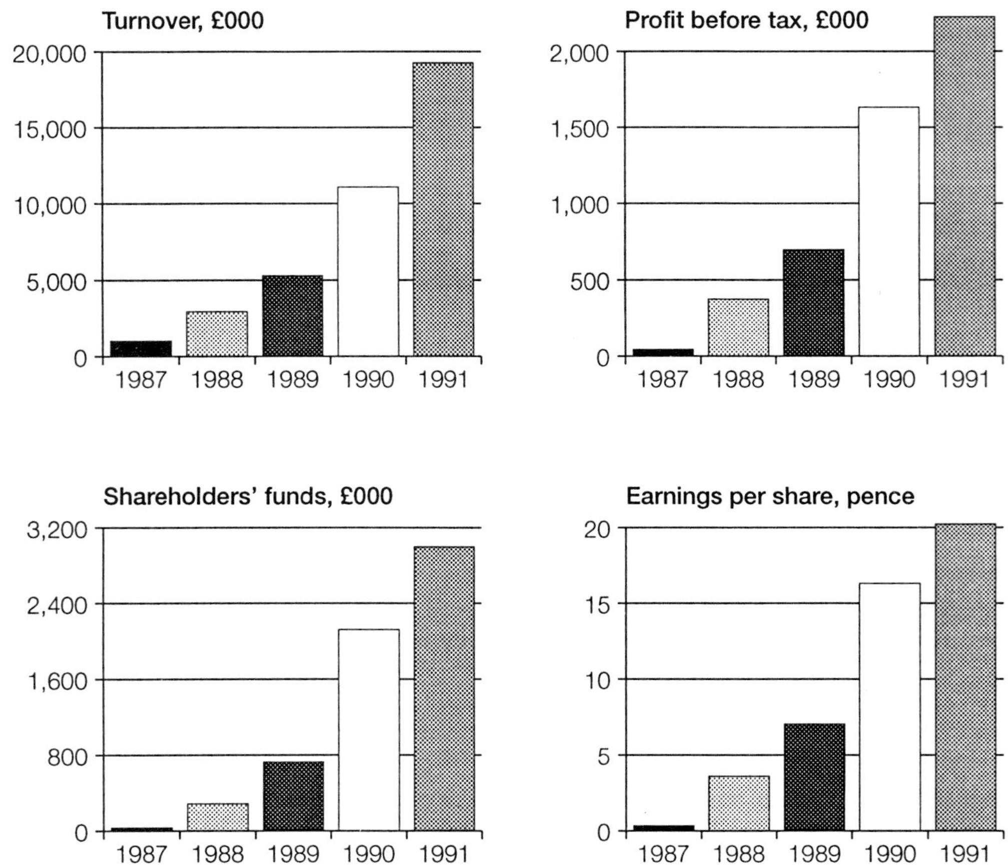

In his statement, the chairman was able to report, in comparison with the previous year:

1. An increase in pre-tax profits of 36 per cent from £1,639,000 to £2,231,000;
2. Increased turnover, up 75 per cent from £11.1 million to £19.4 million;
3. An advance in EPS from 16.3p to 20.2p – an increase of 24 per cent.

The review was full of optimism. In fire protection:

> *'A great number of contracts have been secured from a wide geographical and client base. In particular, there has been a marked increase in the number and value of public and industrial sector projects secured. . . . Despite the slowdown in commercial sector work, [the company] continues to pick up high-value, high-profile office developments.'*

In dry lining:

> *'[The company] has forged ahead and is now established as one of the leading companies in the dry wall industry, capable of undertaking major fast-track projects, [and] continues to concentrate on high-value projects, mainly in the commercial, industrial and public sectors. . . . The market for dry lining remains substantial, and the company's market share is still very small. The opportunities for further growth are therefore considerable.'*

2.2 *The application of SSAP9*

2.2.1 *Long-term contract work in progress*

> *'No area of accounting has produced wider differences in practice than the computation of the amount at which stocks and work in progress are stated in financial accounts.'*

These opening words of SSAP9, *Stocks and Work in Progress*, are of particular relevance to a building company and hence to the object business. The annual financial results of such a company will be made up of a series of contracts, some of which are complete but many of which are ongoing, such that there will frequently be a large component of work in progress (WIP).

This problem is recognised by SSAP9, which suggests that to defer taking profit into account until project completion may result in the profit and loss account only reflecting projects that have been completed during the year, and which therefore would not represent a fair view of corporate activity. SSAP9 suggests that any profit on uncompleted projects taken at the year end needs to reflect the proportion of work carried out at the accounting date, and should also take into account any known (or expected?) inequalities of profitability in the various stages of the project. If it is expected that a loss will result on a contract as a whole, provision should be made (in accordance with the prudence concept) for the whole of that loss as soon as it is recognised.

From a corporate point of view, constant appraisal of the value of WIP in accordance with defined and acceptable principles of good accounting practice is essential if a meaningful and true statement of the company's affairs is to result. This places reliance upon the AIS, yet evidence is all too common within the object company of inconsistent financial reporting and failure to identify the true financial position of ongoing contracts.

2.2.2 *The annual accounts*

Of particular importance in SSAP9 is the note regarding the establishment of profit in an accounting year and the need to match costs with related revenues. If costs are incurred in respect of future revenues, the standard advises that such cost should be carried forward to the next accounting period(s), to be matched with the revenue when it arises. The concept is to match cost and revenue in the year in which the *revenue* arises rather than the year in which the *cost* was incurred.

The effect of these guidelines is that WIP will be stated at cost or, if lower, net realisable value.

It is important that a company states clearly the basis on which stock and WIP have been dealt with in the accounts. The standard suggests that in the case of long-term contract WIP a suitable explanation would be 'at cost plus attributable profit (if any) less foreseeable losses (if any) and progress payments received and receivable.'

The object company's annual accounts indicate the following accounting policy in respect of *turnover and recognition of profit*:

> *'Turnover represents the value of work done including attributable profit. Profit is taken while the contract is in progress having regard to the proportion of the total contract which has been completed at the balance sheet date. Provision is made for foreseeable losses.'*

This, while it appears to comply with the standard, clearly places heavy dependence on the precise manner in which WIP has been valued.

2.3 *The project*

A number of projects are undertaken by the company in any trading year. This paper focuses on the largest project the company has ever undertaken, involving the design and installation of dry-wall lining.

The project was to be completed in 44 weeks commencing in January 1990, and the breakdown of the agreed bid based on performance specification is given in Table 1.

Table 1: Project quotation

	£
Production labour	468,598
Materials	489,350
Site-based overheads	186,384
Total costs	1,144,332
Contribution @ 20%	228,866
Agreed bid	1,373,198

The project started eight months late (not the company's fault – there were delays elsewhere on the main contract), and was actually completed in 80 weeks – an overrun of 36 weeks, as demonstrated in Figure 2.

Figure 2: Project anticipated and actual expenditure profile

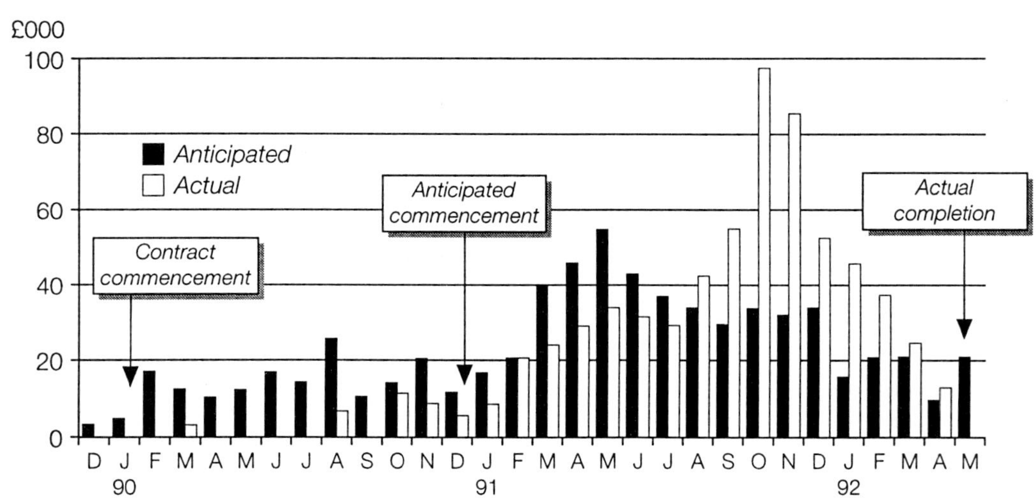

The PM reported over 2,000 changes instructed by the client in the quality, quantity and timing of the project. The cost and value forecast which the PM approved (see project organisation chart, Figure 3) indicated that all the work carried out was 'good' and which, with the application of a higher contribution margin rate of 25 per cent to compensate for direct and consequential effects,[2] suggested a turnover figure of £3,125,000. In actuality, costs in respect of the project had increased by £2,500,000, giving rise to a more correct turnover figure (using the original project contribution) of £3,900,000 (i.e. the £1.4 million of Table 1 plus £2.5 million).

Figure 3: Organisation chart

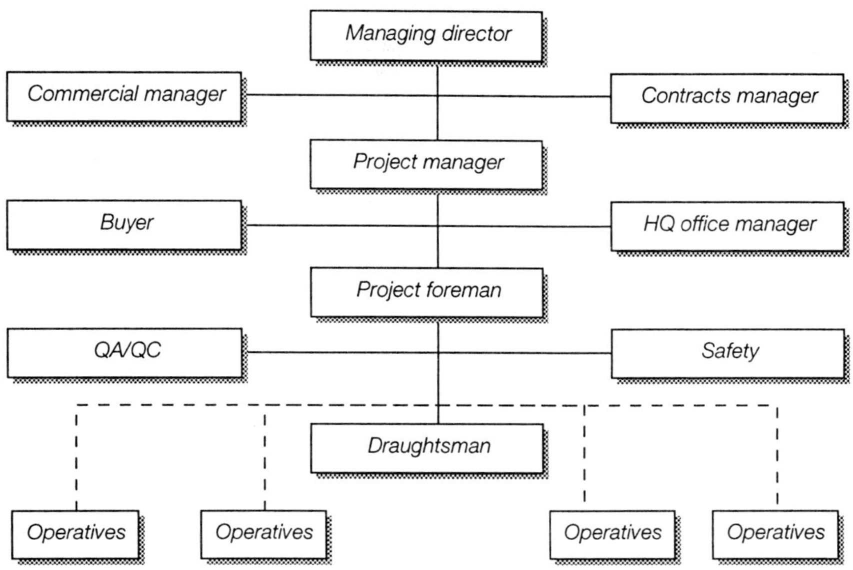

However, it transpired that much of the increased costs were due to the rectification of remedial work, although this was not revealed in the PM's progress reports. *Hopwood* (1972) provides substantial evidence of the 'tricks' employed by managers in manipulation of accounting data. In addition, it is an obvious human trait to tend to suppress information that might be detrimental, or at least perceived as such, to the reporting manager's position (*Read*, 1962).

The client valued the work at only £2,125,000 and insisted that no more money would be paid, counter-claiming defective workmanship in respect of a number of aspects of the project, and the consequent intention to deduct the costs of rectification from the amounts paid over after agreed valuation (see Appendix, Exhibits 1 and 2).

The manner in which the company utilised accounting information for management control and external reporting purposes is represented by the data flow diagram illustrated in Figure 4, with the feedback of cost and value reconciliation data being effected through a system of control documentation.

Figure 4: Cost/value reconciliation in the company's project accounting systems

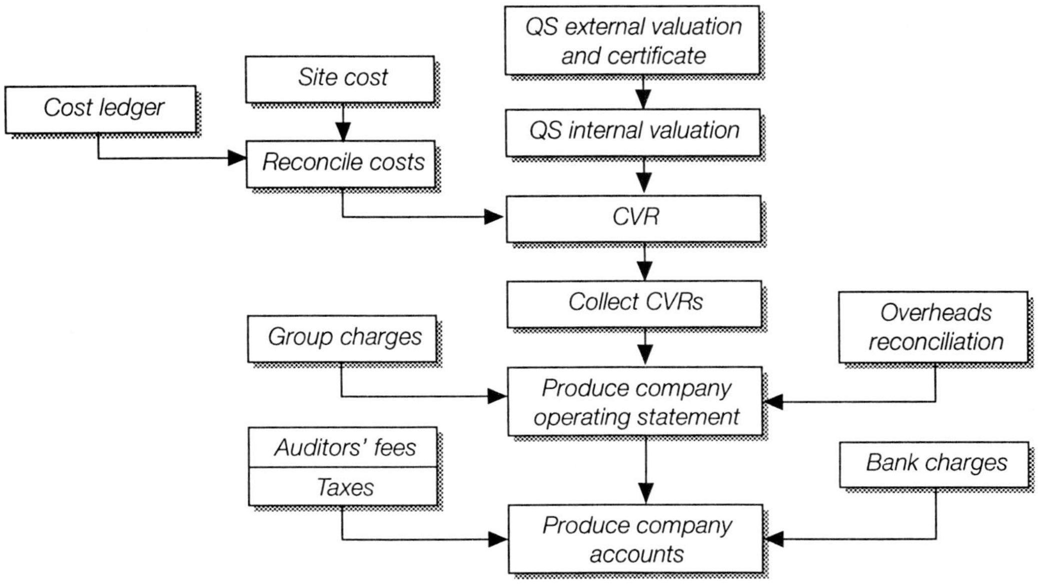

3 *A theoretical perspective on the situation*

3.1 *Unprogrammed and uncertain decisions*

On commencement of a project such as that described, the company is faced with many unknown factors concerning the final outcome of the project in financial terms. The project work scope and specification are often varied in the course of construction, and in consequence disruption of the regular progress of the work takes place, giving rise to claims for additional monies. On this particular project, a total asking price of around £3,900,000 indicated by the accounting records compared with a figure based on cost and value concepts which suggested £3,150,000 as the correct measure of project valuation (even though this subsequently proved fallacious). The latter figure was nevertheless £1 million in excess of what the client considered to be the correct figure. How could this situation arise?

Earl and Hopwood (1980) have suggested that management accounting systems have been designed on the basis that decisions are programmed, although they tend in practice to be used in non-programmed situations. They identify two types of uncertainty: uncertainty about cause and effect relationships, and uncertainty about objectives. Combining these two independent variables gives rise to the four possibilities and suggested solutions illustrated in Figure 5.

Figure 5: Uncertainty, decision-making and ideal information systems

		Uncertainty in objectives	
		Clear objectives	*Ambiguous objectives*
Uncertainty in cause-effect relationship	*Good predictive models*	*Decision by computation: answer machine*	*Decision by compromise: dialogue machine*
	Poor predictive models	*Decision by judgement: learning machine*	*Decision by inspiration: idea machine*

Source: *Emmanuel et al.* (1990), based on *Earl and Hopwood* (1980)

The project had a clear objective (a 20 per cent margin on direct project costs – Table 1) but suffered from inadequate cause and effect determination in that the project was unique – nothing of this scale or complexity had previously been undertaken by the company. There was thus only a poor predictive model available of eventual out-turn, and the company did not know which course of action was likely to yield optimum results. The business was therefore in a classic unprogrammed decision-making environment.

Emmanuel et al. (1990) have proposed that when companies are operating in a non-routine way, then that is the very time when greatest reliance upon accounting measures of performance is likely to occur. In the situation described, such reliance was ill founded.

3.2 *Agency theory*

3.2.1 *The project manager*

The cause behind the problem (which the company also experienced with some of its other on-going projects), may be identified as the inappropriate use and even abuse of the company's conventional AIS for management control purposes in an unprogrammed decision-making environment. The high uncertainty that was involved suggests the possibility of mere accounting numbers providing a less than complete picture of the project's progress (*Hirst*, 1981). *Govindarajan's*

(1984) proposal for a more subjective assessment of managerial performance would appear to have relevance, given the circumstances surrounding the project and the PM's position in relation to it.

To test this hypothesis of abuse of the company's AIS, it is possible to present the employment relations of lower-level managers in the business using an agency framework, although *Tiessen and Waterhouse*'s (1983) identification of the limitations of this approach, particularly that many business organisations are not susceptible to analysis from such a formal contracting point of view, should be borne in mind (as, perhaps, should, at a more basic level, *Choudhury and Walker*'s (1987, p.113) stricture that the complex mathematical expositions of the concept add nothing to basic common sense!).

Emmanuel et al. (1990) may be drawn upon in the whole of this section to illustrate the relevance of agency theory to the company and personalities involved.

In its present state of development, agency theory relates to a single principal and a single agent, and an agency exists whenever one party (the principal) hires another party (the agent) to perform some service (*Kaplan*, 1982). It has been suggested in some quarters (*Baiman*, 1982, and *Sundem*, 1981, by way of example) that, in a more sophisticated form, agency theory could provide a comprehensive theory of management accounting. The suggestion is, however, not without its critics (*Spicer and Ballew*, 1983; *Puxty*, 1993), and such a development would certainly seem a long way off at present. There has, nevertheless, certainly been a shift away from a purely normative approach to management accounting 'towards a concern for explaining observed current practice consistent with rational behaviour on behalf of the parties involved' (*Choudhury and Walker*, 1987, p.101).

Specifically, as *Scapens* (1985) has indicated:

> *'the agency model is used to identify the combination of employment contract and information system that will maximise the utility function of the principal, subject to the behavioural constraints imposed by the self-interest of the agent.'* (p.169)

In the agency model, the principal is also assumed to be motivated by self-interest, but as Scapens (*loc. cit.*) points out, their two sets of 'preferences, beliefs and information' do not have to be congruent.

In the case of the object project, the PM was hired by the MD to perform a task in an uncertain environment ('uncertain' because of the scale and complexity aspects previously indicated). In recognition of this, the principal (MD) delegated decision-making authority to the agent (PM), but owing to the uncertainty surrounding the agent's task, the principal could only observe the agent's efforts to a limited extent.

This removed the element of 'behavioural' control which, for example, *Ouchi*'s (1979) work suggests might have been appropriate in different circumstances.

Relevant information was unevenly distributed between the parties involved and the existence of such information asymmetry meant that the principal had to depend either on communication from the agent or incur monitoring costs to discover whether the agent was actually performing in accordance with the principal's best interests. As was pointed out by *Jensen and Meckling* (1976) in their classic contribution to our understanding of agency theory:

> *'It is generally impossible for the principal . . . at zero cost to ensure that the agent will make optimal decisions from the principal's viewpoint. In most agency relationships the principal and the agent will incur positive monitoring and bonding costs (non-pecuniary as well as pecuniary), and in addition there will be some divergence between the agent's decisions and those decisions which would maximise the welfare of the principal.'* (p.308)

Agency theory offers insight into the appropriateness of the AIS by focusing on the problem of information asymmetry. There are in fact two sets of problems, *moral hazard* and *adverse selection* (see

Macintosh (1994), for some useful observations on these concepts), both of which can be discussed focusing on the project.

3.2.2 *Moral hazard*

Moral hazard (*Perrow* (1986), p.229, discusses the origins of the expression) arose from the MD's remoteness from the project and his consequent reliance upon accounting information as a measure of the effort expended by the PM. The presence of uncertainty made it extremely difficult for the MD to discover whether the difference between the valuation of the project as derived by the AIS, and the payment proposed by the client (at their valuation), was due to uncontrollable external events which would eventually become apparent, or the failure of the PM to take appropriate action in managing the company's assets – hence the interpretation of moral hazard as a form of 'shirking' (*Scapens* (1985), p.172).

This problem has been addressed in recent work by *Robson* (1992), in which he develops the concept of 'action at a distance', suggesting that the use of the numerical metaphor in accounting practice is related to the problem of achieving long-distance control. The more remote the actor (in this case, the MD) is from the settings he wishes to act upon, the more translations[3] need to be mobilised in order to overcome the problem of distance.

The only normative measure the business used to monitor the PM's performance was variance analysis based on the agreed bid (i.e. budgeted) level of contribution. From this it would seem likely that the company was following a somewhat conventional view of the contribution of the AIS to management control within the organisation, in that it assumed (*Emmanuel et al.*, 1990) that:

1. the PM desired certain rewards that the MD could give, such as esteem, increased perquisites, bonuses and promotion;

2. the PM was led to understand that receipt of these rewards would be positively correlated with performance of his division; and

3. the PM was left to maximise his self-interest by attaining or surpassing the performance measures set by the MD.

On the face of it, the possibility of opportunistic behaviour on the part of the PM existed. As *Watts and Zimmerman* (1978, p.113) have commented, 'individuals act to maximise their own utility. In doing so, they are resourceful and innovative.' While the PM's commitment to targeted performance was motivated by the clear connection between 'good' performance and various desired rewards, nevertheless a comparison of the PM's expected and actual performance highlights deviations from plans, which recourse to a better predictive model might perhaps have found ways to avoid.

3.2.3 *Adverse selection*

As *Emmanuel et al.* (1990) have indicated, the concept of adverse selection (see *Perrow,* 1986, for a discussion of the concept) is closely linked to that of moral hazard, but concentrates on pre-decision information, and is the misrepresentation of the true attributes or qualities of the task under consideration, under circumstances in which it is not possible for the other party to determine the truth of what is happening at low cost.

Translating this to the case at hand implies that the effort the PM expended in developing plans and the detail of the predictive model he used could never be perfectly known by the MD. And owing to the superior information (being 'nearer the ground') that the PM had about the operation of his division of which the project was a part, the MD could only guess at the effort required to meet a particular plan or target. The MD would have had to incur considerable cost (any *costless* information would be considered to have positive value, even if imperfect (*Holstrom*, 1970), to determine whether or not the PM's information either intentionally or unintentionally misrepresented reality.

So, while *Emmanuel et al.* (1990, p.170) have suggested that 'The opportunity for bias is constrained by the ability of the senior manager to make his own independent predictions of likely outcomes,' in the case described very little of such ability actually attached to the MD.

Adverse selection therefore focuses on the need for planning and in particular the incentives the PM had to introduce bias and budgetary slack (see Christensen (1982) for a discussion of the implications of agency theory for budgetary participation).

3.3 *The reward structure*

The use of a budget-constrained style of control, based on the PM's ability continually to meet the budget on a short-term basis, appears inconsistent with the company's divisionalised structure.

This rigid style of evaluation, concentrating as it did on the accounting performance measure, represented an attempt to impose a rigid control mechanism in a situation of unprogrammed decision-making. Given the PM's perception that rewards were conditional upon meeting budgeted levels of performance, he might have been motivated, given the duration of the project together with its value and inherent complexity, to indulge in opportunistic behaviour in the short term at least, to ensure that his quarterly performance bonus was maximised, since this was based on the contribution from his division (*Baiman and Demski* (1980a, 1980b), discuss the implications of agency theory for performance evaluation). There would certainly appear to be enough evidence available to counter the alternative proposal that the PM, because of the uncertainty of the situation in which he found himself, simply experienced difficulty in estimating the likely outcome, even though he tried his best (*Peterson and Miller*, 1964). Clearly, in any given situation, the outcome will always depend both on the effort expended by the agent and the realised state of the world (*Scapens* (1985) p.169).

This may account for the fact that the extent of the control loss on the project was not perceived by the MD until it was 75 per cent complete (see Appendix, Exhibit 3).

Behavioural theory suggests that rewards used to motivate managers may result in them adjusting the timing of reports and generally submerging detailed information that may prove harmful to the claiming of a reward (*Read*, 1962). The company has letters on file regarding the project where the client is seriously questioning performance on the project and flagging the clear intention to withhold monies from the progress payments. The content of these letters was neither communicated to the MD at the time nor cognisance taken of them by the PM when feeding back details of actual performance. It could be argued that the PM, in the circumstances, acted in a way that for him represented a rational response to the performance pressures of his situation.

4 *Concepts for an improved AIS*

4.1 *Behaviour congruence*

These findings lend support to a hypothesis focusing on the use and efficacy of a goal congruence approach. Drawing upon *Parker* (1979), the use of the AIS can be summarised as follows.

The problem is that accountants' belief in their responsibility for encouraging goal congruence among managers has its origins in part in their *unitary* view of the business enterprise. However, some organisation theorists (*Sayles*, 1979; *Pettigrew*, 1973) hold to a *pluralist* view of business enterprise, which suggests it comprises a coalition of individuals and groups who co-operate to go some way towards achieving their separate objectives. It can therefore be argued that the company is a coalition of which top management is only a part, and where the whole range of aspirations is continually juggled and balanced.

The movement from a unitary to a coalition view of the firm is largely attributable to the progression of concepts of the firm from those produced by the classical economic and management schools of around 1900–39, to those emanating from the more behavioural perspective of business enterprise generated by more modern organisational theorists from around 1940–70.

The classical economic/management theories of the firm were built upon the principles of division of labour, chain of command, line and staff structures and span of control. The firm was viewed as an entrepreneur seeking to maximise profit by rationally deciding upon courses of action with full knowledge of the available alternatives. This classical perception is limited, however, by its concentration upon the formal structure of the organisation and by its neglect of individual personality, informal groups, intra-firm conflicts and decision processes.

The more modern approach to organisations focuses primarily on the human aspects of organisations and, relying more on empirical research data, investigates strategic parts of the organisation's subsystems, their interrelatedness and their goals. This frame of reference is described as *behavioural* and argues that:

1. the firm itself does not act – only its personnel do so;

2. behaviour is conditioned by personality as well as by environmental factors;

3. behavioural processes of organisation members are a function of their cognitions, perceptions, beliefs and knowledge.

In seeking to promote goal congruence within the organisation (rather than some looser form of co-ordination) the AIS was being used by the object company's financial director to advise the MD by adhering to a predominantly classical view of organisations, and viewing the AIS as being able to 'tell the truth'. However, this would appear to ignore the warning voiced by *Emmanuel et al.* (1990, p.186) that both AIS designers and the senior managers who use their systems should be aware of 'both the technical limitations of accounting measurement procedures and the likely effects of the way in which managers use accounting information'.

The existing AIS was poorly designed for the circumstances in which it was now being expected to work (*Hopwood*, 1972), and incorporating an element of behavioural theory into the control mechanism would perhaps allow the business to be considered more in terms of a goal-, motivation- and equilibrium-seeking and decision-making system (*Schiff and Lewin*, 1970).

4.2 Contingency theory

Given that information provided by the company's AIS tended to be oriented towards the production of outcomes desired by the sender, and in a situation that was complex and/or uncertain, there seemed no obvious way of overcoming its deficiencies. What, therefore, was the way forward?

Contingency theory attempts to explain how the design of an appropriate AIS is placed in the context of organisational response to a wider environment. The effectiveness of the design of the AIS then depends on its being adaptive to changes in external circumstances and internal responses.

The underlying premise of the contingency approach is that there is no universally appropriate AIS that applies equally to all organisations in all circumstances. Nevertheless, it is acknowledged that the AIS has a role to play in maintaining decision-makers' commitment to a feasible region of intersecting acceptable sets of actions.

> *'An analysis of this aim of identifying possible feasible regions of activity and attempting to keep the organisation within them is offered by Thomas (1980). He argues that in the absence of agreed objectives, managers should be encouraged to propose actions that they are willing to take and that are consistent with top management's desires. In other words,* behaviour congruence *(i.e. an agreed set of actions) replaces* goal congruence *(i.e. an agreed set of goals) as a guiding principle'* (Emmanuel et al., 1990, p.196)

Although behaviour congruence is only a general guideline, it has the following specific characteristics that can be applied to business:

- it emphasises the necessity of matching organisational structures to the AIS, so that decision-makers become actively encouraged to implement actions that are beneficial to the whole organisation;

- it makes clear the restraint exercised by organisational controls on incentives for promoting self-interest, and the significance of the AIS in the control process.

The overall intention of a behaviour-congruent AIS is that it should at least deter managers from implementing organisationally undesirable actions. This is clearly a long way from the situation which had become apparent in the object company, where the magnitude of the problem facing it only became visible when letters of complaint from the client began to be sent direct to the MD.

Two examples of opportunistic behaviour may be identified.

- The business was one of historically high growth, and there had been pressure to meet targets to maintain this growth. In their seminal work, *Lowe and Shaw* (1968) identified an implicit belief that sales would continue to grow as one potential source of bias in budget setting, which could well apply in the situation now described. This resulted in the manipulation of the accounting data in the short term, thereby also ensuring a good bonus for the PM. Such an emphasis on the short term to the possible detriment of the long term is not, of course, a phenomenon unique to the object company (*Otley*, 1978);

- The attainment of the company's profit target had been achieved by overvaluing the additional works ordered by the client and thus compromising the annual accounts, as demonstrated by the £1 million unpaid by the client.

The result was the (apparent) maintenance of gross profit, and reported as such, but at the expense of encouraging behaviour that stored up problems for the future. Evidence suggests that by the spring of 1991 those problems had come home to roost.

5 *The company's response*

5.1 *Bolting the stable door*

The company's response to the £1 million deficit in its accounts was the adoption of post-audit investigations into all projects not performing to expectations.

Within the head office cost structure are a number of claims specialists – quantity surveyors whose job it is to compare all projects' outcomes with the original budgets. The idea is then to search for ways (using the contractual agreement) of increasing revenue to match the valuation of the project in the company's (internal) management and (externally) reported accounts. On this basis it was hoped it would eventually be possible to 'negotiate up' the level of payment by the client on the project. Presently, however, the situation was one of accrued profit being held in the accounts without the receipt of the related cash flow.

This post-audit project control behaviour instigated by the MD was directly driven by the degree of change in the works and was seen as a rational response to the opportunistic behaviour of the PM in the manipulation and bias of the financial feedback relating to the project, disguised by the claiming of substantial extra monies allegedly for extra works carried out on an ongoing basis.

However, it is questionable whether this approach of closing the stable door after the horse has bolted provides any sort of long-term solution to the company's problems. As *Cyert and March* (1963) have indicated, problems that are encountered and solved repeatedly tend gradually to be taken over by standardised responses. As a consequence, companies accumulate a repertoire of programmes, particularly in stable environments, and this makes them insensitive to change. Using a standard operating procedure such as a post-audit on problem projects, instead of genuine problem solving, may enable the organisation to devote its (limited) available decision-making resources to problems which are novel and really deserve such attention. However, such an approach in changing environments may lead to organisational inertia, which in the final analysis can threaten survival (*Morgan*, 1986).

It can be postulated that this is the situation in which the company found itself. Since the post-audit approach had been successfully employed in the past to extract extra monies from clients and thus 'square the accounts', it had become cast into an action programme – the more successful it was, the more likely its adoption as a standardised response.

However, the size of the problems associated with the object project provided evidence sufficient to challenge the efficacy of this response – to 'unfreeze' what had perhaps become a standardised response, and to replace it with something new, although probably not as radical as the *Hedberg and Jönsson* (1978) proposal for a semi-confusing information system designed to shake the organisation out of rigid behaviour patterns.

The cash outflow resulting from the project caused the company to apply to its bankers for a £2 million overdraft facility to cover its working capital requirements, and this provided a threshold of counter-evidence to suggest to senior management that change was required. New, ameliorating actions were clearly necessary to organise the business to face up to the environment then perceived by the MD.

This process of development has been modelled based on the idea of 'myth' introduced by *Hedberg and Jönsson* (1977) and reproduced as Figure 6.

Figure 6: Initiators of action in different phases of organisational belief in present policy

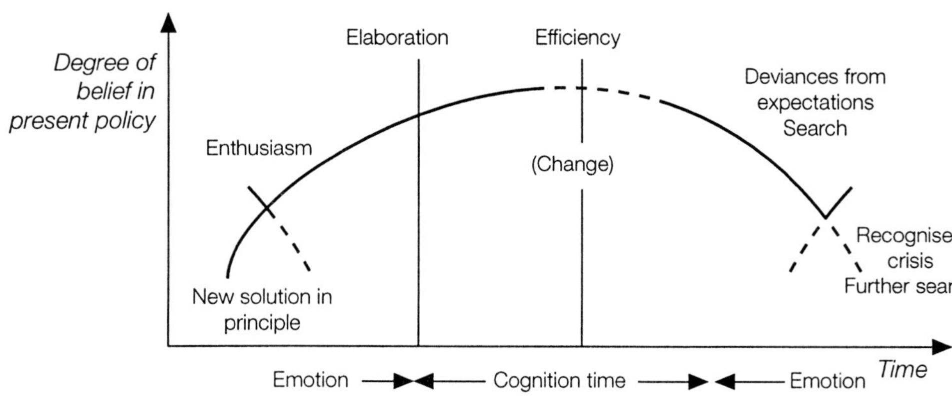

Source: *Hedberg and Jönsson* (1977)

The main proposition is that organisations develop over time on the basis of spurts of enthusiasm, largely based on wishful thinking, that initiate vigorous action. This is followed by a decline in the unifying and directing force of the leading idea, ending in a final decline which ends in crisis. This crisis encourages the company to accept a new strategy without conflict between proponents of the old and new strategies.

The solution considered by the company, and subsequently implemented, was in principal to concentrate on the concept of domain definition, to serve as a forecasting model by top management. The requirement of the AIS was then that it should in tandem assist in controlling the business while the new control procedures gained familiarity.

5.2 *Specific implications for the company's AIS*

The company could no longer 'afford' the conventional AIS it had previously. Its encouragement for managers to mis-record, manipulate and bias data did nothing to promote behaviour congruence, and was driving the company into ineffective project investment decisions and manipulation of the concepts of SSAP9. Hence there appeared to be a *prima facie* case for change.

The long-term success of the company depends upon its ability to take effective project investment decisions. The business is project driven (these are the contribution centres) and is thus a multi-divisional business, giving it some advantage over the unitary form in terms of the quality of decisions it can make. It has the ability, for example, to reallocate resources should an initial project not meet expectations. Therefore, had the problems associated with the project become apparent earlier, action could have been taken to address them. Hence the business may be viewed as a mini-capital market (*Williamson*, 1970), in which top management acts as an allocator of resources.

The loaded question which now needed a response was: could the company's existing (and conventional) AIS be modified to cope with the demands of the solution principle chosen, which was to drive effective project investment decisions in an unprogrammed decision-making context – always bearing in mind the underlying premise of the contingency approach, restated here, that there is *no one universally appropriate AIS that applies equally to all organisations in all circumstances*?

The crucial factor was the provision of feasible feed-forward controls, since, without these, the provision of feedback control in the form of performance measures such as budget variance would be unlikely to lead to effective management control.[4] Motivation and measurement are inextricably linked under conditions of uncertainty, and the knowledge that performance would be measured along certain dimensions provided the motivation for managers to make their performance look good in the interests of self-preservation.

Participation in planning was something tried latterly by the MD, and while this might be criticised as a means merely of allowing managers to secure relatively easy standards of performance (*Hofstede*, 1968), it at least allowed the planning gap between the expectations of the MD and what the PM thought he could 'deliver' to be thoroughly explored.

The AIS could then provide service in assessing how actual events match the assumptions that were made when the plan was developed. Both the MD and the PM may then become more aware of defects in their identification of key variables or their ability to predict how those variables will react in an uncertain environment.

The evaluation process becomes much richer when the actual events and planning assumptions are compared. This is because the assumptions are not totally limited to events that can be measured in financial terms: for example, the meeting of target dates, quality of personnel employed on a project, etc.

The aim of designing the AIS along these contingency lines was, quote, simply to improve learning and to beat the environment rather than to 'beat the PM'!

It seems critically relevant that, while the business is attempting to find a balance so that learning can thrive and experience accumulate (at the same time as excessive integrative complexity and inertia in decision systems are counteracted), the feed-forward controls advocated should include cash flow as a key variable because of its intimate relationship with the identified strain on working capital.

This gave rise to the addition of the cash-flow model illustrated in Figure 7 to supplement the existing AIS. This suggests that the figure the client has actually paid should be used to drive the cost/value reconciliation and the taking of attributable profit or loss, as the case might be.

Figure 7: Cash flow-based contract accounting system

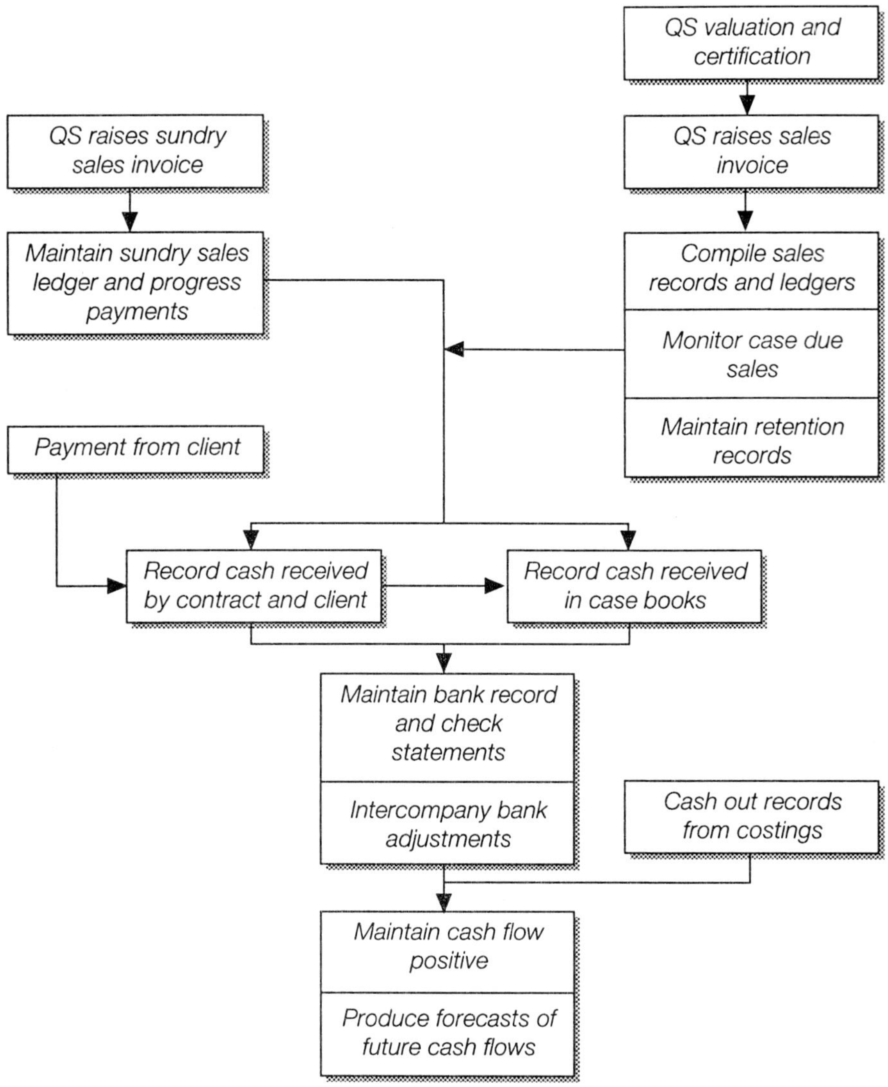

The possibility of manipulation remains, and no doubt the forecasting procedures will require adjustment over time. However, any review should be accompanied by a re-examination of the key assumptions on which the original cash flows were based. The possibility of education then becomes a beneficial result – aligned with the critical success factor of returning the company to a situation of cash positive at the bank. To help reduce the opportunistic behaviour element, weekly co-ordination meetings began to be held in respect of the project dealing with site operations, quantity surveying issues and feedback on SWOT elements (see Appendix, Exhibit 4).

6 Conclusion

Analysis of the company's situation has indicated that the main problem facing it was the valuation of work in progress in respect of project work subcontracted to the company and undertaken largely in 1991, whose size made it of considerable significance. Whereas the annual accounts covering the period, and by application of SSAP9, had utilised a valuation figure which promised some level of eventual profit, the valuation placed on the work by the client was some £1 million lower – a figure which suggested no level of profit at all on a full cost basis.

This difference of opinion may be explained in terms of:

(i) substandard work requiring rectification not picked up by the AIS (or concealed by the PM), but which the client (the lead contractor) was refusing to pay for;

(ii) many additions by the client to the original work specification, for which the company was seeking reimbursement.

The MD's physical remoteness from the project placed great reliance upon information produced by the AIS. However, this would retrospectively appear to have provided an inadequate measure of results. The company's reward structure suggested the possibility of opportunistic behaviour on the part of the PM responsible for the project, leading to the potential for bias and budgetary slack which the MD was unlikely to be able to detect because of the 'novel' nature of the project and his inability to monitor the effort expended by the PM without additional cost. In the circumstances, the efficacy of the model being used to predict eventual outcome was also brought into question.

While goal congruence may have been perceived by the accountants within the company to come about automatically from a 'correct' utilisation of the AIS, this depended upon a *unitary* view of corporate behaviour being reality. A more *pluralistic* view of the organisation would lend weight to a coalition view of events. However, given the potential orientation of the AIS towards the production of outcomes that were more desired by the sender than the recipient, the way forward was difficult to discern given the complex and/or uncertain situation in which the company found itself.

Concentration on the development of appropriate patterns of *behaviour* congruence, in preference to previous attempts (via the AIS) at mere *goal* congruence, appeared to offer some promise of a way forward.

The overall conclusion reached by the research is that the historic AIS used by the company was inadequate in the situation of uncertain decision-making which surrounded the particular project. Feedback from the AIS in terms of the 'cost' and 'value' concepts of project control proved inadequate because the project was 'novel', thereby giving rise to inadequate cause and effect determination. Proposals for a behaviour-congruent AIS, now adopted by the company, have been provided.

As has been indicated elsewhere, 'All descriptions of human situations are necessarily partial and incomplete. All of us . . . construct our own versions of reality even when we strive to be as "objective" as possible' (*Easton*, 1992, p.3). Nevertheless, the sequence of events portrayed above has been recorded as accurately as possible, and it is firmly believed that the interpretation placed upon them by the present authors is the correct one. However, 'remedies' are another matter, and only time will tell whether the prescriptions for improvement achieve the desired effect.

7 Postscript

7.1 1991/92 accounts

The company's annual accounts for the year to 29 February 1992, the highlights of which are given in Figure 8, revealed a starkly difference situation from that of a year previously.

Figure 8: Company profile 1992

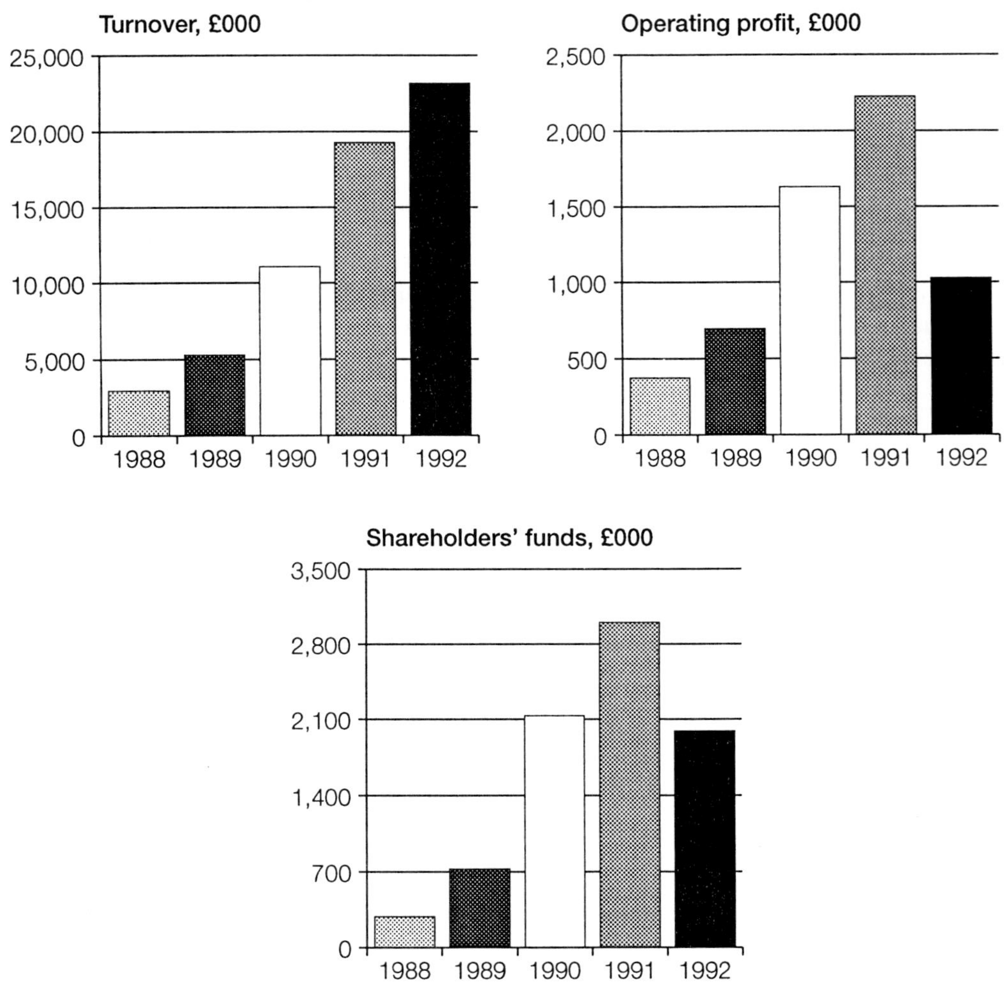

While 1991–92 turnover increased, a loss after taxation of £948,000 was recorded, compared with a profit of £1,438,000 in 1991. The directors felt unable to recommend a final dividend.

Included in the chairman's statement was the comment:

> *'We have decided to make exceptional provisions for [a contract in] the UK due to the protracted nature of the dispute. . . . In line with other contractors we have experienced a lengthening period of debtor collection which has moved the Group into a borrowing position.'*

At this time, the total claim before the client in respect of the project had grown to £6.2 million, as indicated in Table 2.

Table 2: Revised project claim

	£m
Original agreed bid	1.4
Variations	2.8
Claim for breach of contract and disruption	2.0
	6.2

7.2 1992–93 accounts

Even when the accounts for yet another year were published (to 28 February 1993), the dispute with the client was still not settled. At that time, the client had offered a sum of only £2 million (and this was the figure at which the project's value was then carried in the company's books), comprising their valuation of the work estimated at £3 million, less £1 million in respect of liquidated damages due to a penalty extracted by the ultimate client because of delays in the overall project. At that time, the company estimated its incurred *prime cost alone* at £3.5 million.

The following note appeared:

> *'Since the year end the Group has issued an arbitration notice against [the client] in respect of a substantial final account in respect of the "—" project. The Directors consider the Group will be successful in its claim, having taken account of all counterclaims and having obtained legal and other professional advice. However, given the nature of such claims it is difficult to accurately estimate the amounts ultimately recoverable, and therefore the directors have included in the financial statements an amount lower than the amount of its claim. Professional costs to complete the arbitration process have also been provided.'*

7.3 Capital restructuring – October 1994

A legal hearing of the dispute was scheduled for February 1995. Meanwhile, at the end of October 1994, the company offered issues of both ordinary and preference shares to, among other things, reduce the bank debt previously referred to. It was indicated that without this restructuring the company might be unable to continue to trade. The offer documentation indicated that arbitration proceedings in respect of the project had been settled:

> *'In order to maintain cash flow, it has been necessary to concede discounts to achieve settlement of outstanding debts. This includes the "—" project . . . in respect of which the Company was engaged in arbitration proceedings against "—" The Board considered it necessary to accept a significantly lower amount than that carried in the Company's accounts to settle this claim.'*

The company's results for the year to 28 February 1994 were announced at the same time as the share offer. These showed a £1.684 million pre-tax loss arising from the settlement.

Notes

1. The term 'case study' is used in the *Easton* (1992, p. 1) sense of 'the intensive study, description and analysis of a person, group or organisation from which theory can be derived or by which theory can be tested' (*Bromley* (1986) summarises these different uses), although 'illustrated' might be a better descriptor in present circumstances.

2. The bulk of a contractor's profit can often stem from extra works negotiated with the client (see, for example, *Lock* (1992), Ch. 15; *Harrison* (1992), Ch. 6), particularly in a recession when the tendered bid will probably have been 'tight'.

3. 'Translations' means constructions between the inscription and the events, objects and activities to which it refers.

4. This assumes that variance analysis is an effective control instrument, and thoughts on this vary (for example, see *Hofstede* (1968) who thought that adverse budget variances indicate that the 'system' is working properly, and should accordingly not be used to attribute blame).

References

Baiman, S. (1982), 'Agency research in managerial accounting: a survey', *Journal of Accounting Literature*, Spring, pp. 154–213.

Baiman, S. and Demski, J.S. (1980a), 'Variance analysis procedures as motivation devices', *Management Science*, 26, August, pp. 840–848.

Baiman, S. and Demski, J.S. (1980b), 'Economically optimal performance evaluation and control systems', *Journal of Accounting Research Supplement*, 18, pp. 184–220.

Bromley, D.B. (1986), *The Case Study Method in Psychology and Related Disciplines*, John Wiley: Chichester.

Choudhury, N. and Walker, M. (1987), 'Agency theory and management accounting – a critique', in Arnold, J., Scapens, R. and Cooper, D. (eds.), *Management Accounting: Expanding the Horizons*, Vol. 3, Chartered Institute of Management Accountants Occasional Papers Series, CIMA: London, pp. 61–121.

Christensen, J. (1982), 'The determination of performance standards and participation', *Journal of Accounting Research*, 20, pp. 589–603.

Cyert, R.M. and March, J.G. (1963), *A Behavioural Theory of the Firm*, Prentice-Hall: Hemel Hempstead.

Earl, M.J. and Hopwood, A.G. (1980), 'From management information to information management', in Lucas, H.C., Jr., et al. (eds.), *The Information Systems Environment*, North-Holland: Amsterdam.

Easton, G. (1992), *Learning from Case Studies* (2nd edn), Prentice-Hall: Hemel Hempstead.

Emmanuel, C., Otley, D. and Merchant, K. (1990), *Accounting for Management Control* (2nd edn), Chapman & Hall: London.

Govindarajan, V. (1984), 'Appropriateness of accounting data in performance evaluation: an empirical examination of environmental uncertainty as an intervening variable', *Accounting, Organizations and Society*, 9, 2, pp. 125–35.

Harrison, F.L. (1992), *Advanced Project Management* (3rd edn), Gower: Aldershot.

Hedberg, B. and Jonsson, S. (1977), 'Strategy formulation as a discontinuous process', *International Studies of Management and Organisation*.

Hedberg, B. and Jonsson, S. (1978), 'Designing semi-confusing information systems for organisations in changing environments,' *Accounting, Organizations and Society*, 3, 1, pp. 47–64.

Hirst, K.K. (1981), 'Accounting information and the evaluation of subordinate performance', *The Accounting Review*, 56, 4, pp. 771–84.

Hofstede, G.H. (1968), *The Game of Budget Control*, Tavistock: London.

Holström, B. (1979), 'Moral hazard and observability', *Bell Journal of Economics*, Spring, pp. 74–91.

Hopwood, A.G. (1972), 'An empirical study of the role of accounting data in performance evaluation', *Empirical Research in Accounting*, supplement to *Journal of Accounting Research*, 10, pp. 156–82.

Jensen, M.C. and Meckling, W.H. (1976), 'Theory of the firm: managerial behaviour, agency costs and ownership structure', *Journal of Financial Economics*, 3, pp. 305–60.

Kaplan , R.S. (1982), *Advanced Management Accounting*, Prentice-Hall: Englewood Cliffs, N.J.

Lock, D. (1992), *Project Management* (5th edn), Gower: Aldershot.

Lowe, E.A. and Shaw, R.W. (1968), 'An analysis of managerial biasing: evidence from a company's budgeting process', *Journal of Management Studies*, 5, pp. 304–15.

Macintosh, N.B. (1994), *Management Accounting and Control Systems: an Organizational and Behavioural Approach*, Wiley: Chichester.

Morgan, G. (1986), *Images of Organisation*, Sage: Beverly Hills, Calif.

Otley, D.T. (1978), 'Budget use and managerial performance', *Journal of Accounting Research*, 16, pp. 122–49.

Ouchi, W.G. (1979), 'A conceptual framework for the design of organisation control mechanisms', *Management Science*, 25, September, pp. 833–48.

Parker, L.D. (1979), 'Divisional performance measurement: beyond an exclusive profit test', *Accounting and Business Research*, 36, pp. 309–19

Perrow, C. (1986), *Complex Organisations: a Critical Essay* (3rd edn), Random House: N.Y.

Peterson, C. and Miller, A. (1964), 'Mode, median and mean as optimal strategies', *Journal of Experimental Psychology*, 68, pp. 363–7.

Pettigrew, A.M. (1973), *The Politics of Organizational Decision-making*, Tavistock: London.

Puxty, A.G. (1993), *The Social and Organizational Context of Management Accounting*, Chartered Institute of Management Accountants Advanced Management Accounting and Finance Series, CIMA: London.

Read, W.H. (1962), 'Upward communication in industrial hierarchies', *Human Relations*, 15, February, pp. 3–16.

Robson, K. (1992), 'Accounting numbers as "inscription": action at a distance and the development of accounting', *Accounting,Organizations and Society*, 17, 7, pp. 685–708.

Sayles, L.R. (1979), *Leadership*, McGraw-Hill: New York.

Scapens, R.W. (1985), *Management Accounting: A Review of Recent Developments*, Macmillan: Basingstoke.

Schiff, M. and Lewin, A.Y. (1970), 'The impact of people on budgets', *The Accounting Review*, 45, 2, pp. 259–68.

Spicer, B.H. and Ballew, V. (1983), 'Management accounting systems and the economics of internal organisation', *Accounting, Organizations and Society*, 8, 1 pp. 73–96.

Sundem, G.L. (1981), *Future perspectives in management accounting research*, paper presented at Seventh Accounting Research Convocation, University of Alabama.

Thomas, A.L. (1980), *A Behavioural Analysis of Joint-Cost Allocation and Transfer Pricing*, Stipes: Champagne, Ill.

Tiessen, P. and Waterhouse, J.H. (1983), 'Towards a descriptive theory of management accounting', *Accounting, Organizations and Society*, 8, 2/3, pp. 251–67.

Watts, R.L. and Zimmerman, J.L. (1978), 'Towards a positive theory of the determination of accounting standards', *The Accounting Review*, 53, 1, pp. 112–34.

Williamson, O.E. (1970), *Corporate Control and Business Behaviour*, Prentice-Hall: Englewood Cliffs, N.J.

Appendix

Exhibit 1

Facsimile transmission from the client to the company

Subject: '—' Project

Date: 9 May 1991

The costs of defective works relating to the above project are as follows:

7120 – Dry lining	£50,000
3110 – Fire protection	£25,000

These monies will be deducted from this month's valuation.

Exhibit 2

Memorandum from the client to the company

Subject: Core B2 – Walls not plumb

Date: 16 July 1991

Further to your handover of core B2, we have identified a number of walls that have been erected out of plumb (walls shown on attached). The relevant levels are listed below:

(i) 3rd floor, first flight down – wall not plumb on either side of movement joint.

(ii) 4th floor, first flight down – ditto.

(iii) 2nd floor, first flight down – ditto.

(iv) 1st floor, first flight down – ditto.

This is preventing the wall from being fixed correctly. Your immediate action is required to rectify these defects.

Exhibit 3

Memo from the managing director to the contracts manager

Subject: '—' Project: actions required

Date: 16 September 1991

1. According to the recent report compiled by '—', up to 50 per cent of the wage bill may be being paid out to take account of 'remedials'. If this is so, then the Contracts Department

are either unaware of the extent of the problem or people are telling their superiors what they want to hear. From today's date a report must be prepared *every week,* detailing the costs and percentages of the wage bill which is down to 'remedials'. Do not leave this report on desk-tops.

2. I am unhappy with the apparent reluctance of our senior contracts people to release the 'ineffective supervisors' and recruit people of a higher calibre. It appears at every opportunity we protect the people who are allowing *bad* work to be erected. It is these people who will govern the success of their superiors! I presume the two supervisors 'surplus to requirements' detailed in your report to me of 13th instant have now gone.

3. '—' has been directed to site. I presume he has been 'set out' and directed in achieving the goal of getting the fire protection installation approved and ticked off.

4. It appears to me that we are making the mistake of forming a structure on site where we put 'names into boxes' and assume they are doing the business. Clearly, they are not.

5. [The client] has informed me that [a firm of consultants] will remain on site until such time that we have a QA/QC operation that breathes confidence into the team on site. This does not mean a wonderful paper system but a system where the work that is erected is checked and rejected if incorrect (now there's a thought!). With [the consultants] on site this week, a written proposal must be prepared and tabled to me before 20th instant so that on 23rd it can be put to [the client). I would suggest that the supervisors sign the QA/QC sheet in addition to the QA/QC manager. This will *not* compromise their position. Erection and passing of substandard work will compromise their position as it will yours and mine if we continue to almost condone the current regime.

6. Stephen Squires has been appointed on a *temporary basis* to compile a claim and further better particulars on both packages. Stephen will be the 'historics' man while '—' will be the present and future man. I will chair a meeting on Wednesday on site to direct and minute the actions required.

7. [The client] has agreed, in the interim, to pay for the 20 extra fixers deployed to site. A report must be submitted to [the client] every day detailing the 20 fixers, where they have been working, hours on site, *not* materials used, and headed 'For Record Purposes Only'. We will then on a weekly basis submit a cost report to [the client).

8. Weekly allocation sheets and reports detailing why and where we cannot build in line with the 30.8.91 programme must continue to be submitted to [the client] on a weekly basis.

9. By the end of September 1991 the contracts goal is to get [the consultants] off site by having quality work erected and passed or rejected if inferior with the *supervisors* signing of the work with a QA/QC manager collating and submitting the reports to [the client). Submit the reports with defective work being passed and we will stand no chance of gaining confidence or winning the battle.

Commercially, by 5 October 1991, we need to have submitted further and better particulars to enhance the payments to date.

I will see you and '—', together with Stephen Squires, on site on Wednesday.

Signed: MD

Exhibit 4

Memo from SS (project claims specialist) to various parties

Subject: '—' Project: co-ordination meeting

Date: 9 April 1992

I propose to hold a weekly co-ordination meeting at 10.30 a.m. on Tuesday of each week to monitor and control [the project], starting Tuesday 14.4.92.

The venue for the meeting will be the [project's] QS office in Holborn.

I propose an agenda as follows:

1.0 *Site operations*
- 1.1 Number of men on site and costs
- 1.2 Forecast of labour requirements and costs
- 1.3 Schedule of cost drivers
- 1.4 Gaps in information
- 1.5 Task-driven objectives

2.0 *Quantity surveying*
- 2.1 Gaps in [the company's] accounts
- 2.2 Forecast of cash to be paid by client
- 2.3 Contractual problems
- 2.4 Gaps in information
- 2.5 Task-driven objectives

3.0 *Feedback*
Feedback on recent meetings, jungle drums, etc. to allow the crystallisation of our present strengths, weaknesses, opportunities and threats and the adoption therefore of a common objective and a programme of actions to be agreed.

Finally, minutes will be taken.

Regards,

SS

Managers' Performance-related Compensation and Corporate Performance in Large French Industrial Companies

Pascal Langevin
(Lyon Graduate School of Business)

Managers' Performance-related Compensation and Corporate Performance in Large French Industrial Companies

Introduction

The purpose of this paper is twofold. First, it presents empirical results on compensation and performance evaluation systems employed in large French industrial companies. This is an interesting issue; little literature has been produced on French practices . Second, this paper presents the empirical testing, in a management accounting context, of two theoretical results of the principal–agent model. The results show that higher overall corporate performance is related to greater use of profit-sharing schemes attributed to divisional managers according to budgeted performance realisation.

The first section presents the theoretical results of the agency model tested in this research. The operationalisation of the model and the method used are provided in the second section. The third section presents the results, which are then discussed in the last section.

Agency model theoretical results

The agency theory considers a company to be a group of rational agents acting in their self-interest (*Jenson and Meckling*, 1976). The theory usually studies the relationship between a principal who delegates some decision-making responsibility to an agent. Since the principal's and agent's interests may not be convergent, the principal has to determine a contractual arrangement that satisfies both parties. This contractual arrangement combines a compensation function and an information system. Thus this performance-related compensation system is determined in such a way that the principal's utility is maximised when the agent has also maximised his own utility.

Two types of agency relationships referring to performance-related compensation systems are empirically studied in the managerial literature. The first is concerned with the relationship existing between shareholders and the top management of a firm (*Tosi and Gomez-Mejia*, 1989; *Abowd*, 1990; *Gerhart and Milkovich*, 1990; *Jensen and Murphy*, 1990). The second is concerned with the relationship between the firm's top management and managers to whom top management has delegated responsibilities (*Govindarajan and Gupta*, 1985; *Gerhart and Milkovich*, 1990; *Kahn and Sherer*, 1990; *Leonard*, 1990; *Fisher and Govindarajan*, 1992). The empirical research presented in this paper takes place in this latter context. It examines the relation between corporate performance and managers' compensation and performance evaluation systems. Here, 'managers' are of two types depending upon the company structure. In divisionalised companies, managers are divisional managers while, in non-divisionalised companies, staff managers are considered.

As *Jensen* (1983) noticed, two different approaches have been developed in agency theory.

The positive theory of agency tries to explain the existence and the form of contractual arrangements observed in organisations. This paper follows this positive approach to study some compensation systems employed in the sample companies. The purpose of the second approach, namely the normative theory of agency or principal–agent theory, is to determine the characteristics of optimal contracts to be implemented in order to lessen agency problems. In what is called the basic model (*Baiman*, 1982), the principal hires for a single period a single agent whose action (or effort), together with a state of the world, generate a pay-off to the firm (that is, to the principal). Two results of this basic model are examined in this study.

- When the pay-off is the only observable signal, the agent can explain a low pay-off due to his own action by an unfavourable state of the world. This problem is known as the moral hazard problem; *Shavell* (1979) showed that this problem can be solved by employing risk-sharing contracts. In other words, the compensation must depend upon the pay-off.
- When a signal or the agent's action is available, *Homstrom* (1979) indicated that this signal must be included in the compensation function to improve the solution. In other words, it is better to relate compensation to a performance measure.

This research tries to test these two theoretical results using the method described below.

Research method

Sample and data collection

The sample was taken from the SCRL data base.[1] To limit potential problems due to uncontrolled activity variables, the sample was only composed of industrial companies. Moreover, in order to increase the probability of finding developed compensation systems and divisionalised structures, large companies were selected, size being defined by turnover and payroll. Since a 10 per cent response rate was targeted (a usual figure in French surveys) and to limit the resort to non-parametric tests, a sample of 1,200 companies was needed. Therefore, selecting industrial companies having a turnover larger than 250 million francs and a payroll over 250, a final sample of 1,260 companies was obtained.

Two data sources were used. Data concerning corporate performance were derived from the SCRL database. All other data were obtained by questionnaire. Since this study considers that top management has to determine performance-related compensation systems to overcome agency problems, the questionnaire was sent to the 1,260 CEOs. Returned questionnaires totalled 136 (a 10.8 per cent response rate), of which 133 were used in the data analysis. Although this response rate might seem low, it is a common figure in French surveys. Therefore, there is no reason to think that a non-response bias might exist or to question the representativeness of the sample.

Variables operationalisation and measurement

Four variables were employed in this research.

Pay-off

This study considers top management to be the principal. It is then necessary to determine what top management's pay-off is. Two opposing theses appear in the literature concerning top management's goals. The economic thesis considers top management's objective to be profit (*Lewellen and Huntsman*, 1970; *Masson*, 1971; *Benston*, 1975), while the managerial thesis considers it to be size (*Ciscel*, 1974; *Cosh*, 1975). Several studies have shown that both criteria are frequently mixed (*Simon*, 1983; *Coughlan and Schmidt*, 1985; *Murphy*, 1985; *Gomez-Mejia et al.*, 1987). Three corporate performance criteria were used therefore in this research to measure the pay-off. Return on equity (ROE) and return on assets (ROA) refer to the economic thesis, while turnover growth rate (TGR) refers to the managerial thesis. Accounting measures were used because the sample included unlisted companies for which market values were not available. Finally, to limit problems due to exceptional events, the mean values computed over the last four years were taken.

Agent's compensation

French executives' compensation can be split into six components:

- basic salary
- cash bonus
- stock bonus
- stock options
- fringe benefits
- pension plans and contingency funds (above the minimum level imposed by law).

French people do not speak easily about their own remuneration, nor even about their subordinates' compensation. It was therefore not conceivable to get answers about managers' compensation. Consequently, only the compensation structure was analysed in this research. This compensation structure was measured by asking the respondent for the percentage of each component in the average manager's total compensation.

Information signal

The use of an information signal to determine the agent's compensation, as defined in the model, refers to the performance evaluation systems. These systems have long been studied in the literature (for example: *Solomons*, 1965; *Franck*, 1979; *Brownell*, 1982; *Govindarajan*, 1984; *Kaplan*, 1984; *Scapens and Sale*, 1985; *Ezzamel*, 1992). Many criteria are employed in these systems. Since it would have been difficult to deal with numerous criteria or even to select particular ones, five general indicators were used in this research:

- *Corporate performance indicator*. This indicator does not give information about the agent's effort but about the pay-off. It allows one to consider the profit-sharing schemes. It refers to corporate performance as a whole and not to individual performances, as do the next two.
- *Unit performance indicator*. This indicator measures the absolute performance of an individual or a unit managed by this individual (i.e. a divisionalised unit or a staff department).
- *Budgeted performance realisation indicator*. This criterion is concerned with the manager's performance compared with a budgeted standard of performance.
- *Manager's appraisal indicator*. Contrary to the previous two, this indicator refers to subjective methods of evaluation.
- *Human capital indicator*. This additional item allows one to take into account all criteria which do not correspond to those above, namely education level, position, age, tenure. These criteria are not contained in the agency model. Nevertheless, they are probably employed when determining some compensation components (e.g. base salary).

To measure this information signal, the respondent was asked how important the use of each indicator (corporate performance, unit performance . . .) is in the determination of each component (base salary, bonus . . .) of managers' total compensation. The importance is valued on a six-point Likert scale (from 1 'not important at all' to 6 'very important').

It was then possible to compute a score measuring the overall importance of each indicator. For example, the score measuring the overall importance of 'corporate performance' in determining the manager's total compensation was computed in the following way:

$$\text{EVG} = \sum C_i G_i$$

where C_i is the percentage of component i in the manager's total compensation and G_i is the importance of the use of the 'corporate performance' indicator in determining component i.

Divisionalisation

Considering that this study is concerned with the basic model results, that is, concerned with the relationship between a single principal and a single agent, divisionalisation may be a controlling variable. Compared with a staff manager, a division manager can more easily be said to be a single agent, since his decisions may be less dependent upon other division managers' decisions. Moreover, this research investigated corporate performance. Numerous studies have considered the relationship between divisionalisation and performance, and showed an effect (*Armour and Teece*, 1978; *Hill and Pickering*, 1986; *Hoskisson*, 1987). It was therefore important to include this controlling variable in the research.

To measure this divisionalisation variable, the respondent was asked to indicate if his company is divisionalised or not. The consistency of the answer was checked by additional questions concerning decision power, external and internal constraints, information circulation and information specificity. No inconsistency was noticed in the answers.

Hypotheses

As has been said, two hypotheses were tested. They correspond with the two theoretical results presented above and are displayed in Table 1. The general idea was that corporate performance increases when one goes from hypothesis 1 to hypothesis 2.

Table 1: Theoretical results and operationalised hypotheses

Theoretical hypotheses	*Operationalised hypotheses*
R1 *Shavell* (1979): Risk-sharing contracts increase the principal's utility.	*H1* Companies employing profit-sharing schemes to compensate managers have higher corporate performance.
R2 *Holmstrom* (1979): Risk-sharing contracts containing information on the agent's effort are Pareto-superior to risk-sharing contracts which only depend upon pay-off.	*H2* Companies where profit-sharing schemes also depend upon managers' performance evaluation have higher corporate performance.

Results

Descriptive analysis

Controlling variables

The sample is composed of 116 (87 per cent) companies employing between 250 and 5,000 people. It has a good representativeness on a sectoral basis. The 90 divisionalised companies are significantly larger than the 43 non-divisionalised ones (α<0.1 per cent, χ^2 test).

Corporate performance

Results concerning corporate performance are given in Table 2. A very large dispersion of realised performance can be observed.

Table 2: Corporate performance in the sample

Performance Measure	*Mean*	*SD*
Return on assets	10.80%	84.12%
Return on equity	11.48%	48.50%
Turnover growth rate	12.16%	55.00%

No significant differences were observed which depended upon size and divisionalisation.

Compensation

'Base salary' and 'cash bonus' are the two main components of the managers' total compensation in the sample (see Table 3).

Table 3: Compensation components in the sample

Compensation component	*Number of companies employing this component*	*Mean*	*SD*
Base salary	133 (100%)	82.30%	10.54%
Cash bonus	112 (84%)	13.92%	8.03%
Stock bonus	6 (5%)	4.93%	2.53%
Stock options	23 (17%)	5.90%	6.07%
Fringe benefits	65 (49%)	5.47%	3.45%
Pension plans	45 (34%)	6.12%	4.21%

Significant differences in compensation structure were found which depended on size and structure. Small companies make a greater use of 'base salary' whereas large companies employ 'stock options' and 'pension plans' more (α<0.5 per cent, variance analysis). Moreover, 'cash bonuses' are employed more by divisionalised companies (14 per cent against 8 per cent of total compensation) while non-divisionalised companies make a greater use of 'base salary' (87 per cent against 80 per cent of total compensation). These differences are significant (α<0.1 per cent, t-test).

These results seem consistent with agency theory. When top management finds it difficult to control managers, as in the case of large and/or divisionalised companies, incentive compensation systems are employed. Moreover, these incentive schemes appear to be effective. Corporate performance is higher in companies employing variable compensation systems (regrouping 'cash bonus', 'stock bonus' and 'stock options') than in companies using fixed compensation schemes (regrouping 'base salary', 'fringe benefits' and 'pension plans'). The t-test or the Mann–Whitney U-test were used, depending on the sub-samples' size. All tests are in the hypothesised direction and five out of nine are significant (See Table 4).

Table 4: Corporate performance and fixed versus variable compensation (significance level of differences being in the hypothesised direction)

	Whole sample	*Divisionalised companies*	*Non-divisionalised companies*
ROA	0.4%	2.4%	0.9%
ROE	1.5%	3.9%	6.0%
TGR	16.0%	10.0%	17.0%

Performance evaluation systems

The performance evaluation indicators employed in the determination of each component of compensation are displayed in Table 5.

Table 5: Performance evaluation indicators employed to determine each compensation component (1 < indicator value < 6)

	Corporate performance	*Unit performance*	*Budgeted performance realisation*	*Manager's appraisal*	*Human capital*
Base salary	2.58	3.02	3.16	4.71	3.15
Cash bonus	4.02	3.52	3.74	2.67	1.10
Stock bonus	6.00	0.40	0.40	0.40	1.40
Stock-options	3.53	1.74	1.95	1.89	2.68
Fringe benefits	1.33	1.46	1.21	1.74	3.46
Pension plans	1.51	0.74	0.38	0.56	2.56

It can be observed that one (or several) indicators is (are) more important for each component. To test this observation, the value of the most important indicator was compared with the mean of other regrouped indicators, using a t-test or a Wilcoxon matched-pairs signed-rank test, depending upon the sample size. The results are shown in Table 6 (the test for the 'stock options' component was not possible, since there were fewer than eight companies).

Table 6: Main indicators employed to determine the compensation components

Compensation components	*Number of companies concerned*	*Main indicator*	*Mean value of main indicator*	*Aggregated mean of other indicators*	*Student's t or Wilcoxon's T*	$\alpha/2$
Base salary	133	Manager's appraisal	4.71	2.98	t = 12.23	<0.1%
Cash bonus	112	Corporate performance	4.02	2.76	t = 5.25	<0.1%
Stock bonus	23	Corporate performance	3.53	2.07	T = 54	<0.5%
Fringe benefits	65	Human capital indicator	3.46	1.43	t = 5.30	<0.1%
Pension plans	45	Human capital indicator	2.56	0.80	t = 4.84	<0.1%

All differences are significant. These results do not change when divisionalised and non-divisionalised companies' sub-samples are investigated.[2] In such circumstances one indicator is much more important in the determination of each component, but this indicator is not necessarily unique, as another look at Table 5 shows:

- Base salary takes into account all indicators in an important way.
- Cash bonus is also determined with the help of individual performance indicators.
- Stock bonus and stock options are determined by overall 'corporate performance', but only for a given status ('human capital' indicator).
- Fringe benefits are strongly dependent upon 'human capital' but without neglecting all other indicators.
- Pension plans need a good 'corporate performance' to be attributed.

If one now considers the performance evaluation scores computed as previously described, one can observe that the 'manager's appraisal' score is employed the most in determining the manager's total compensation, while 'corporate performance' and 'human capital' scores are employed the least (see Table 7).

Table 7: Performance evaluation scores in the sample (1 < score value < 6)

Code	*Performance evaluation score*	*Mean*	*SD*
EVG	Corporate performance	2.74	1.61
EVL	Unit performance	3.00	1.92
EVO	Budgeted performance realisation	3.14	1.82
EVA	Manager's appraisal	4.30	1.22
EVD	Human capital	2.91	1.74

Size does not induce any significant difference in the choice between performance evaluation systems. On the other hand, the divisionalised companies use more 'corporate performance' and 'individual performance' systems than do non-divisionalised companies (see Table 8).

Table 8: Performance evaluation scores in divisionalised versus non divisionalised companies (means and student's t)

	Non-divisionalised companies	*divisionalised companies*	*t*	*α*
EVG	2.27	2.96	–2.39	1.73%
EVL	2.30	3.34	–2.93	0.41%
EVO	2.67	3.36	–1.97	4.86%
EVA	4.34	4.29	0.26	79.30%
EVD	2.93	2.89	0.12	89.90%

Considering these results, it can be thought that top management needs to resort to local performance measures to motivate divisional managers, and to overall corporate performance systems as a means of converging top management's and manager's interests.

Traditional systems such as 'human capital' and 'appraisal', on the other hand, are not employed differently in the two types of company. One explanation could be that these systems are not suitable for dealing with agency problems encountered in divisionalised companies, but they are still used to comply with usages or to meet other objectives.

Tests of hypotheses

Both hypotheses were tested using the same methodology. It consisted of tests for difference of means. The general aim was to investigate if a given performance-related compensation system is associated with a higher overall corporate performance. For each hypothesis, the same process was used as follows:

- divide the sample into two sub-samples of the same size. This division was based on the performance-related compensation score corresponding to the hypothesis tested.
- compute the mean overall corporate performance of each sub-sample.
- test the difference of the means using a t-test or a Mann–Whitney U-test, depending upon the sub-samples' size. One-sided tests were used, since the hypothesis imposed the sign of the relation.
- go to the next hypothesis by dividing one of the two sub-samples into two new sub-samples.

For each hypothesis, this process was executed using the whole sample first, then using the divisionalised companies sample, and lastly using the non-divisionalised companies sample.

Test of hypothesis 1: Profit-sharing

A company is said to have a profit-sharing scheme when the 'corporate performance' indicator is important in the determination of important components of managers' total compensation (i.e. when the 'EVG' score is high). Thus the 'EVG' variable was used to divide the sample. Most of the results (six out of nine) were found to be in the expected direction, but not with a significant level. Therefore, in the sample, companies employing profit-sharing schemes do not perform significantly better than companies which do not use such a compensation system.

Test of hypothesis 2: Individual performance evaluation

A company is said to take into account information on the agent's effort when it employs in an important way 'unit performance', 'budgeted performance realisation' or 'manager's appraisal' indicators to determine important components of managers' total compensation (i.e. when 'EVL', 'EVO' or 'EVA' scores are high).

To test this hypothesis, the samples of companies employing profit-sharing schemes were divided into two sub-samples using 'EVL', 'EVO' and 'EVA' scores in turn as division variables. Results are displayed in Table 9.

Table 9: Significance levels of tests of hypothesis 2 (only results being in the expected direction are displayed)

All sample (two sub-samples of 33 companies) (t-test)

	EVL	EVO	EVA
ROA	50%	15%	25%
ROE	37%	13%	28%
TGR	-	-	25%

Divisionalised companies sample (two sub-samples of 22 companies) (U-test)

	EVL	EVO	EVA
ROA	13%	5%	30%
ROE	10%	4%	24%
TGR	–	5%	30%

Non-divisionalised companies sample (two sub-samples of 10 companies) (U-test)

	EVL	EVO	EVA
ROA	–	–	–
ROE	–	–	–
TGR	> 5%	–	–

Most of the results have the expected sign in the whole sample (seven out of nine) and in the divisionalised companies sample (eight out of nine). This is not the case in the non-divisionalised companies sample (only one out of nine). Moreover, in the divisionalised companies, three results are significant, with the 'EVO' variable and the three corporate performance measures (ROE, ROA, TGR). Therefore, divisionalised companies employing compensation systems based on budgeted performance realisation have higher performance levels than those which do not resort to these compensation systems. One may think that these systems are necessary to control the autonomy of divisional managers and to get their interests consistent with those of top management.

Discussion and concluding remarks

This research demonstrates the predictive power of the agency model. Where agency problems might be important, namely in large divisonalised companies, variable compensation and performance-related compensation systems are employed more often than in other types of company. On the other hand, results concerning the prescriptive power of the model are less significant. Here we refer to the hypotheses which state that these incentive systems increase the overall corporate performance.

Testing hypothesis 1 has shown that a higher corporate performance is related to the use of profit-sharing schemes, but without statistical significance. This lack of significance might be explained by the absence of relative measures and contingent variables. Is it possible to measure performance in an absolute way, or must it be relative to some standard? Would the consideration of activity, diversification level, management style etc. have improved the results? Those are interesting questions to be addressed in subsequent researches.

The testing of hypothesis 2 has shown that the use of profit-sharing schemes based on local performance indicators is related to higher corporate performance. This relation is significant in divisionalised companies employing the 'budgeted performance realisation' indicator. In agency theory terms, when a strong agency relationship exists (divisionalisation), profit-sharing contracts employing a signal on the agent's effort (budgeted performance realisation indicator) are related to a higher principal's utility (corporate performance).

Nevertheless, one must be careful in the interpretation of this result. No causal relationship has been demonstrated. Are incentive systems inducing higher performance, or is it because the company has a high performance level that it can pay additional compensations to managers? A time-series analysis might answer this question.

Several methodological problems may have occurred in this research. It has already been noticed that the representativeness of the sample is not verified.

Additionally, the basic model refers to a single agent. Better results being obtained in divisionalised companies, it seems that this was appropriate. Nevertheless, it does not necessarily mean that no agency problem exists with staff managers. Moreover, what does happen when the divisions are strongly interrelated? Theoretical extensions of the principal–agent model to teams should be considered in subsequent research to investigate these issues (*Baiman and Demski*, 1980 and 1986; *Holmström*, 1982).

The basic model also refers to a single period, but without indicating how long a period is. What is important in the model is the sequence of events: the principal determines the compensation function, the agent selects his effort level, the pay-off is realised, finally the agent is paid. The research did not consider this difficult issue, and a cross-sectional analysis was used. Since the implementation of incentive systems may take time to produce its effects, it may again be thought that a time-series analysis would have been more appropriate. Nevertheless, this method would not completely solve the sequence problem just discussed. Finally, the basic model is based on ex-ante relationships, while the survey used ex-post measures of performance.

In spite of these methodological problems, this research provided at least three contributions:

- thorough examination of the operationalisation of the agency model, its hypotheses and its results. This study thus produced some tests of these results.
- observation of the predictive power of the agency model in a managerial accounting context.
- data concerning performance-related compensation systems employed in large industrial French companies.

Further studies either inside companies or on samples with different features (size, activity, ownership etc.) would improve understanding of the relationships. Additional important variables might thus be discovered and then be considered in the subsequent development of the theoretical model.

Notes

1. The SCRL database contains the annual accounts of 260, 000 French registered companies. It also includes general information (e.g. workforce, CEO's name, address etc.) and about 150 financial criteria. This database is updated every six months.

2. Except for 'fringe benefits' and 'pension plans' components in non-divisionalised companies where the significance level is not reached.

References

Abowd, J.M. (1990), 'Does Performance-Based Managerial Compensation Affect Corporate Performance?', *Industrial and Labor Relations Review*, Vol. 43, Special Issue, February, pp. 52–73.

Armour, H.O. and Teece, D.J. (1978), 'Organizational Structure and Economic Performance: a Test of the Multidivisional Hypothesis', *The Bell Journal of Economics*, Vol. 9, No.1, Spring, pp. 106–122.

Baiman, S. (1982), 'Agency Research in Managerial Accounting: a Survey', *Journal of Accounting Literature*, Vol. 1, pp. 154–213.

Baiman, S. and Demski, J.S. (1980), 'Economically Optimal Performance Evaluation and Control System', *Journal of Accounting Research*, Vol. 18, Supplement, pp. 184–220.

Baiman, S. and Demski, J.S. (1986), 'An Empirical Investigation of the Relative Performance Evaluation of Corporate Executives', *Journal of Accounting Research*, Vol. 24, No. 1, Spring, pp. 1–39.

Benston, G.J. (1985), 'The Self-Serving Hypothesis : Some Evidence', *Journal of Accounting and Economics*, Vol. 7, No. 1–3, April, pp. 67–84.

Brownell, P. (1982), 'The Role of Accounting Data in Performance Evaluation, Budgetary Participation, and Organizational Effectiveness', *Journal of Accounting Research*, Vol. 20, No. 1, Spring, pp. 12–27.

Ciscel, D.H. (1974), 'Determinants of Executive Compensation', *Souther Economic Journal*, Vol. 40, No. 4, April, pp. 613–617.

Cosh, A. (1975), 'The Remuneration of Chief Executives in the United Kingdom', *The Economic Journal*, March, pp. 75–94.

Coughlan, A.T. and Schmidt, R.M. (1985), 'Executive Compensation, Management Turnover, and Firm Performance', *Journal of Accounting and Economics*, Vol. 7, No. 3–4, April, pp. 43–66.

Ezzamel, M. (1992), *Business Unit and Divisional Performance Measurement*, CIMA, London: Academic Press.

Fisher, J and Govindarajan, V. (1992), 'Profit Center Manager Compensation: An Examination of Market, Political and Human Capital Factors', *Strategic Management Journal*, Vol. 13, March, pp. 205–217.

Franck, G. (1979), 'Enquete sur les pratiques de gestion du personnel des entreprises dans l'environnement francais', *Les cahiers de recherche du CESA*, No. 128bis.

Gerhart, B. and Milkovich, G.T. (1990), 'Organizational Differences in Managerial Compensation and Financial Performance', *Academy of Management Journal*, Vol. 33, No. 4, pp. 663–691.

Gomez-Mejia, L.R., Tosi, H. and Hinkin,T. (1987), 'Managerial Control, Performance, and Executive Compensation', *Academy of Management Journal*, Vol. 30, No. 1, pp. 51–70.

Govindarajan, V. (1984), 'Appropriateness of Accounting Data in Performance Evaluation: An Empirical Examination of Environmental Uncertainty as an Intervening Variable', *Accounting, Organisations and Society*, Vol. 9, No. 2, pp. 125–135.

Govindarajan, V.A. and Gupta, K. (1985), 'Linking Control System to Business Unit Strategy : Impact on Performance', *Accounting, Organisations and Society*, Vol. 10, No. 1, pp. 51–66.

Hill, C.W.L. and Pickering, J.F. (1986), 'Divisionalisation, Decentralization and Performance of Large United Kingdom Companies', *Journal of Management Studies*, Vol. 23, No. 1, January, pp. 26–50.

Holmstrom, B. (1979), 'Moral Hazard and Observability', *The Bell Journal of Economics*, Vol. 10, No. 1, Spring, pp. 74–91.

Holmstrom, B. (1982), 'Moral Hazard in Teams', *The Bell Journal of Economics*, Vol. 13, No. 3, Autumn, pp. 324–340.

Hoskisson, R.E. (1987), 'Multidivisional Structure and Performance : the Contingency of Diversification Strategy', *Academy of Management Journal*, Vol. 30, No. 4, December, pp. 625–644.

Jensen, M.C. (1983), 'Organization Theory and Methodology', *The Accounting Review*, Vol. LVIII, No. 2, April, pp. 319–339.

Jensen, M.C. and Meckling, W. (1976), 'Theory of the Firm : Managerial Behaviour, Agency Costs and Ownership Structure', *Journal of Financial Economics* 3, October, pp. 305–360.

Jensen, M.C. and Murphy, K.J. (1990), 'Performance Pay ad Top-Management Incentives', *Journal of Political Economy*, Vol. 98, No. 2, pp. 225–264.

Kahn, L.M. and Sherer, P.D. (1990), 'Contingent Pay and Managerial Performance', *Industrial and Labor Relations Review*, Vol. 43, Special Issue, February, pp. 107–120.

Kaplan, R.S. (1984), 'The Evolution of Management Accounting', *The Accounting Review*, Vol. LIX, No. 3, July, pp. 390–418.

Leonard, J.S. (1990), 'Executive Pay and Firm Performance', *Industrial and Labor Relations Review*, Vol. 43, Special Issue, February, pp. 13–29.

Lewellen, W.G. and Huntsman, B. (1970), 'Managerial Pay and Corporate Performance', *American Economic Review*, Vol. 60, No. 3, June, pp. 710–720.

Masson, R.T. (1971), 'Executive Motivations, Earnings, and Consequent Equity Performance', *Journal of Political Economy*, Vol. 79, November, pp. 1278–1292.

Murphy, K.J. (1985), 'Corporate Performance and Managerial Remuneration', *Journal of Accounting and Economics*, Vol. 7, No. 1-3, April, pp. 11–42.

Scapens, R.W. and Sale, J.T. (1985), 'An International Study of Accounting Practices in Divisionalised Companies and Their Associations with Organizational Variables', *The Accounting Review*, Vol. LX, No. 2, April, pp. 231–247.

Shavell, S. (1979), 'Risk Sharing and Incentives in the Principal and Agent Relationship', *The Bell Journal of Economics*, Vol. 10, No. 1, Spring, pp. 55–73.

Simon, D.T. (1983), *Compensation Effects and Accounting Changes : An Empirical Examination*, Ph.D. Dissertation, Northwestern University, Evanston Illinois, June.

Solomons, D. (1965), *Divisional Performance : Measurement and Control*, New York: Financial Executives Research Foundation.

Tosi, H.L. and Gomez-Mejia, L.R. (1989), 'The Decoupling of CEO Pay and Performance : An Agency Theory Perspective', *Administrative Science Quarterly*, Vol. 34, No. 2, June, pp. 169-189.